ON
TOUR

ALSO BY BRADLEY WIGGINS:
IN PURSUIT OF GLORY

TO GEORGE

ON TOUR

BRADLEY WIGGINS

PHOTOGRAPHS BY SCOTT MITCHELL

This edition first published in Great Britain in 2010 by Orion Books
an imprint of the Orion Publishing Group Ltd
Orion House, 5 Upper St Martin's Lane,
London WC2H 9EA
An Hachette UK Company

10 9 8 7 6 5 4 3 2

A CIP catalogue record for this book is available
from the British Library.

ISBN: 9 781 4091 3136 6

Designed by Richard Norgate
Printed and bound in Spain

The Orion Publishing Group's policy is to use papers that are natural, renewable
and recyclable and made from wood grown in sustainable forests. The logging
and manufacturing processes are expected to conform to the environmental
regulations of the country of origin.

Every effort has been made to fulfil requirements with regard to reproducing
copyright material. The author and publisher will be glad to rectify any omissions
at the earliest opportunity.

www.orionbooks.co.uk

INTRODUCTION

THIS is a Tour de France book of sorts, the pictures and the narrative certainly revolve loosely around the events of the 2010 Tour de France, which proved a particularly tough one for me personally. To my mind, July 2010 was the first really big public failure of my career, when I performed well below what I had expected and hoped. The race also offered a steep learning curve for my new Team Sky, who were making their Tour de France debuts. We finished the Tour much wiser men.

But I'm hoping this book is more than just that. My intention right from the outset – regardless of whether I challenged for a podium place and yellow jersey in Paris or trailed home in the bunch – was to offer a comprehensive snapshot of modern-day Grand Tour cycling, or any major stage race for that matter. This effectively is our office, where we go to work and earn a living, where hopes and bodies are cruelly smashed but where, every so often, you have one of those days – and it's not always when you cross the line first – that makes everything worthwhile and keeps you coming back for more.

I love bike racing with a passion. Occasionally I loathe it as well, but mostly it's a mad love affair. It's the whole scene that first drew me in and I don't feel any different now. It's the sheer madness and 'foreignness' of racing on the Continent; the larger-than-life characters that seem to populate the sport, the daily hustle and bustle and that sense of being in a bubble and nothing else mattering. You can lose yourself totally in the sport. It's akin to a travelling circus and the sensation is of being constantly on the move and on tour. That brings the almost daily excitement of arrival and the novelty of a different town and a new hotel. And then, just as suddenly, you are packing your bags again the next morning, handing over your key card at reception and getting a police escort in the team bus to the next start. It's a little bit rock and roll and, if we are honest, that's part of the appeal. You do your stuff and move on to the next gig, the next venue.

Dates and times aren't really how you measure your progress through a long tour and, indeed, the season; they all tend to merge. What you remember are the hotels, good or bad, and occasionally the names of the towns and cities where something significant happened. You remember where you got a good kicking or died a hundred deaths on the final climb, or that blissful day when you miraculously found some form and scarcely broke sweat as you effortlessly tapped your way around some remote corner of France. You always remember where you were when you got ill and where you spent your so-called days off.

As a professional cyclist, you are on the road constantly, on or off the bike. It's a lifestyle as much as a profession and can be very hard, but very addictive and comforting for those who know nothing else. It might not look like it but there is a routine and rhythm, you know weeks in advance what you will be eating and where. All the small daily decisions of life are made by others. You don't have to work the satnav or park the team bus, wash your bike or do the washing. You never have to make the bed and hang the towels up in the bathroom before you leave. Mobile phones and laptops are laid on for you, Skype is set up for you to speak to the wife and kids back home, breakfast is laid out just so every morning, ditto the evening meal. They never vary, you don't have to fret over what to eat. Equally you know exactly what is expected of you on the bike and what the daily task is. Your job is to execute that where possible.

Of course it's not quite as cosy as I make out. Professional cycling is a bloody competitive and dog-eat-dog world, and, yes, we have had our drug cheats who sometimes rip the heart out of the sport and make you question everything you do – although I like to think their days are numbered. We are always trying to get one over the other teams, verbally and on the road, but despite it all we are also a large family and there are a lot of really good friendships between 'opposition' riders and staff as well. In a cycling career you can be involved with three or four teams – I have actually clocked up seven teams, if you include the Linda McCartney racing team which closed down a few weeks after I joined; although I like to think the two

events were not related. Some ex-riders can find it very difficult to tear themselves away from it all when the time comes and I'm not surprised. It's the life they know and understand.

The Tour de France, especially, becomes a daily soap opera, with star names and bit players all making their contribution. It's the ultimate reality TV I suppose, and fans have their favourites even though they know they will never win. Individuals are on edge and there can be a lot of unpredictable and erratic behaviour. The Tour is a massive media event that gets reported around the world with arguments and incidents – sometimes unbelievably petty – getting blown out of proportion. But that only adds to the drama and the feeling that, for three weeks, we are at the centre of the universe. For three weeks it feels like the world is revolving around us guys in the peloton and nothing much

else exists. Complete nonsense of course, but it's quite a heady feeling.

The Tour is also about men – well, mainly men, although every team has women among their back-up staff these days – living together in close proximity and trying to get on together for well over three weeks under a whole load of physical stress and mental pressure. It's a bonanza for people-watchers. It's about dealing with insane tiredness and the emotional roller-coaster that is bike racing. There are plenty of tears around; there is one team out there most days having a complete nightmare. It's about suffering and somehow getting the job done when probably the more logical and sensible option is to sit up, get off and book the first flight home to your loved ones. It's about making decisions on the hoof and then having to deal with the consequences of those decisions, right or

wrong. It's about fronting up to your team-mates if you have been found wanting or lacking bottle, and admitting that you can not always pass the buck.

You could go on almost endlessly. There are extremes of weather to contend with, nature to observe, terrain to respect and mountains to fear. On the Tour de France the three weeks stretch endlessly ahead into the distance. You never really feel – or at least a wise man doesn't – that you are going to reach the finish until you climb off your bike on the final Saturday and sit down with your team that night for a blow-out dinner with just the promenade into Paris left.

All those highs and lows – you just have to try and flatten them out if you are going to survive. You can't live your life like that, you have to try and tread the middle path. Don't despair after the latest nightmare day but equally don't for one minute

think you have the race cracked on the much rarer high days, when you walk on air and your feet hardly touch the pedals. I would advise humility at all times. The Tour de France will always have the final say and accepting that totally is a big step in the right direction. Having made that quantum leap, just keep your head down and try and ride to your limit as often as possible.

You don't have to hype the Tour – just about everything you read is true. It is undoubtedly faster and harder and bigger than any other race in the world. Nearly 200 of the world's best cyclists devote the entire year to arriving in France early every July in peak condition. Nobody is soft pedalling or riding for training on the Tour, it's full-on from start to finish. Even the so called quiet days are harder and faster than quiet days in other races.

It's like 21 consecutive world championships or

one-day Classics virtually on the bounce, give or take two rest days. After riding it for the first time in 2006 I vowed I would never ride it again. I can remember sitting in the village in Morzine after the final rest day promising myself that I would never tackle this race again. It was just so bloody hard. There are sports scientists who say a hard-ridden Tour de France can take three years off your life. And yet here I am again. You very quickly forget the bad days and remember only the amazing buzz of riding in the peloton.

Every day feels like an Olympic final, and I feel qualified to say that because I have competed in my fair share of Olympic finals. The crowds take your breath away, every time. In terms of the profile of the sport, you can bundle everything that happens

in the other 49 weeks of the year together and it still doesn't equal what the three weeks of the Tour offers up. Months later – years later – you wake up in the middle of the night and find yourself suddenly re-living a particular moment from a past Tour as your long dammed-up memories start to come flooding through. Your brain can't take it all in at the time, there is too much going on to assimilate everything. But it is there for you to hit the recall button in later years.

I love reading old Tour books and leafing through all the cycling mags, and one of the aspects that appeals is that nostalgic retro, timeless look that black and white pictures give you. To my mind, there is a very strong link between the old and the new – the bikes may have changed but

the riders certainly haven't – they are still flesh and bone, warriors with their own strengths and weaknesses and stories to tell. The mountains remain constant and great stages present pretty much the same challenges as always. When you leaf back through the pages you can appreciate exactly what the legends – Coppi, Anquetil, Merckx, Hinault, Indurain and, more recently, Lemond and Armstrong – achieved because you have trodden in their footsteps many times. It's the same with the British pioneers who blazed a trail for those of us who followed – fantastic riders like Brian Robinson, Tom Simpson, Barry Hoban, Robert Millar and Sean Yates. Every time I ride up Mont Ventoux I automatically think of Tom Simpson, never more than in 2009 when I was clinging on desperately, hoping to sneak past Lance and get on the podium in Paris the next day.

There is a great feeling of continuity in cycling because we have all ridden the same routes and on the same roads, and with that in mind I asked my friend Scott Mitchell, a professional photographer and fellow Mod, whose take on life I enjoy, simply to tag along with us at Team Sky and snap what he saw on the Tour de France in black and white. Scott is not a cycling fan and, most importantly to my mind, not a specialist sports photographer. He arrived on the Tour completely fresh, although, like the rest of us, he left Paris completely bolloxed. That's the essence of this book. When I get the urge I will also break off and give you my take on a few of the great riders and personalities involved, and hopefully the result will be that elusive timeless snapshot of life on the road I'm talking about. It's time we got this Tour under way.

ROTTERDAM

Hotel Carlton Oasis – Spijkenisse
Also in residence: Crevelo and BBOX
Bouygues Telecom

WELL, I won't do that again in a hurry. What was I thinking of? All my competitive career I have taken the rough with the smooth in prologues and time-trials. Sometimes you are lucky with the weather and the wind and you get an advantage against some opponents, other times it all goes pear-shaped. I lost the final time-trial of the 2009 Giro by a second because the course in Rome suddenly became as slippery as an ice-rink after a later shower. Bad luck Brad. At this year's Giro the Sky team got absolutely battered by a full-scale storm halfway around the team time-trial and still came home second. Without the bad weather that day undoubtedly we would have won handily. Bad luck

again Brad. But I normally take the philosophical view that, over a career, these things even themselves out.

Today at the prologue in Rotterdam it went pear-shaped again for me, but this time we – I – contributed in a big way by trying to box clever, too clever. All our weather data at Team Sky predicted a dry start to the 8.9 km prologue, but with heavy squally showers coming through the second half of the day. An early starter might gain a considerable advantage. It was just possible that Team Sky could mark our Tour de France debut with something very special indeed and we decided I would take a punt and go for one of the earlier start times. As it happened, the rain arrived much earlier than expected and by the time most of the big guns went out – the time I should really have been starting – the road had dried considerably and was noticeably

quicker. An old fashioned cock-up really.

Having clearly got it wrong and fretting over that I then rode very conservatively, anxious in my first season as team leader not to crash with over 3500 km still to go, and finished a pretty undistinguished 77th! – a full 56 seconds behind Fabian Cancellara. I'm angry inside but can't really complain because I bought fully into the idea of trying to get on the front foot and being aggressive. Sky want to be proactive on their Tour debut and make things happen. I am up for that and there is a perfectionist streak in me that fully understands how and why Sky and Dave Brailsford (DaveB) were trying to get an edge. All my Olympic campaigns, with DaveB very much involved, have been painstakingly mapped out and planned to the nth degree, with everything taken into account and the result has been three gold medals and some shrapnel

besides. Those big track medals and world records didn't just arrive by accident, they were planned for, but sometimes in road racing you have to just go with the flow.

I'm a good prologue rider – in fact, with all due modesty, I'm a bloody good prologue rider. I'm top five material and better – and I have missed a golden chance to get in the mix from the off. That was so important at last year's Tour, when I took third in the prologue and then Team Garmin finished runners-up in the team time-trial. I immediately figured near the top of the GC (General Classification) standings and started to build momentum and confidence. I started riding like a race contender right from the off.

It wasn't all bad for Sky today. Geraint Thomas – G – produced a stormer to come fifth and Edvald Boasson Hagan (EBH) must be pleased with his

ninth spot after his injury problems so there were consolations for the team ... but none at all for me. Again with all due respect to both my colleagues, I am a better prologue rider and Tour de France time-triallist than they currently are. Yet I am languishing in 77th! A real low and we aren't even in France yet.

I've been anxious and a bit fretful in Rotterdam this week, not like last year when I just rocked up to the Départ in Monaco with a vague desire to finish top 20 in GC but, above all else, to help team leader Christian Vande Velde onto the podium in Paris. Back in 2009 I remember finishing the British National Road Race on the Sunday before the Tour started and feeling so good and relaxed about life that we stopped on the way home and I blew out with a big pizza and necked a couple of bottles of Corona. Happy days, and why not? During the Tour

itself we would often treat ourselves to a glass of wine in the evening as well. Just the one, but a nice lingering glass of something good to chill out at the day's end. This year I've been living like a monk. I've become completely obsessive and a bit of a grumpy sod as well, so I understand from my wife Cath and long-standing friends. Am I losing my sense of humour? God, that would be awful – you need it to survive in this business. I need to lighten up a bit but this desire to excel for Sky – and myself – and ultimately achieve something historic in the Tour is beginning to eat away at me. Hopefully it will settle down once we get into the rhythm of the race. That's normally the way. Let's get out of Rotterdam, let's get out of this hotel, and get this Tour under way.

Although I'm 30 now, it all seems very new and, in fairness, this is still only my fourth Tour de France. We are clearly a new team and a lot of people are very keen, and anxious, to play their part fully, but there are too many voices in my ear at present, everybody wants to have their say, make their contribution to the team effort. It's all well intentioned but it's information overload sometimes. We need to keep it simple.

Tour Départs are always fraught. They can look so glamorous on TV, and so far I've done Strasbourg, London, Monaco and now Rotterdam, so they spread it around. It's a big gathering point for the entire bike industry and for the fans, officials and sponsors. There is a lively social scene kicking off in the background and, for the press, big stories often rear their head. But for the riders – like any athletes – we just want to make a start. Commentators talk glibly about the romance of the Tour but, as you potter around in your hotel during the days before the prologue, it really dawns on you that nearly 3600 km of brutal cycling await you over the next three weeks and it is you who has got to push the pedals every single inch of the way. It can be a bit of an overwhelming, almost lonely feeling.

Only myself, Michael Barry and Steve Cummings remain from the team that raced together for three weeks in the foul weather in Italy, when we built up a great team spirit. The Giro was a brilliant, crazy, race this year, ridiculously hard at times. We had no luck at all and we all suffered, but by the end of the race were very close and dealing with everything together as a team. It was a good time – you could feel everything coming together for when we were blessed with a bit more luck. With different people on board for the Tour that's been diluted now, and we need to try and build it up quickly.

We are sitting around the hotel here with the guys from Cervelo and BBOX Bouygues. The Tour organisers ASO book up all the team hotels months in advance – in fact it's the way the new route each year generally leaks out to the media before it is officially announced – and then place the teams in those hotels in strict rota. You get what you are given, five stars or no stars. Over the three and a half weeks ASO try to ensure it evens itself out but, being human, you always think the other teams are getting preferential treatment. The grass is always greener, isn't it? We have done all right here but I don't particularly like the look of some on our itinerary in the next couple of weeks. Got to blank that thought out though. Bottom line is that all I need is a comfortable bed to sleep in and Sky have arranged for our own special mattresses and pillows (with integrated ipods, would you believe, if you want to be lulled off to sleep), which they transport from hotel to hotel. Sleep is the absolute must on every Tour, the only way your body stands any chance of recovering. And good, safe, food. Sky have our own chef along, so we should be ok on that score as well.

Just taken delivery of the Tour de France roadbook – the Bible – with all the race routes and stage profiles. To borrow the old cliché, I go from day to day. If you start looking at those real bastard days in the Alps and Pyrenees now, you will just psych yourself out completely. The only way to stay sane is simply to study the day ahead, deal with that, rest and recover. And then go again.

Difficult race to read this one. Alberto Contador is obviously the thoroughbred in the field, but he hasn't been cracking this season, by his own standards anyway. Alberto is still favourite but he is vulnerable. Andy Schleck is a star in the making but has raced very little and needs to improve his time-trialling; brother Frank could be dangerous and looked in very good form wining the Tour de Suisse the other week, but it's Lance who intrigues me. When he came back in 2009 I didn't think he had a chance, what with being out for four years and that bad shoulder injury he picked up in the spring. Yet he came third. This time he seems to have peaked much better and looked in seriously good nick in the Tour de Suisse. He looked very impressive in the prologue here today when he finished fourth, just behind Dave Millar and just ahead of G. Lance may be heading for 39 but he is lean and fit. The Lance of old, to my eyes. I would be pretty fearful

of him because Radioshack are a strong team who will back him to the hilt.

Rode around the prologue course at practice this morning with Mark Cavendish, my old mate. We are like brothers really, and because of that we have the occasional ruck, but we've enjoyed a nice mellow year this time around. Mark's had a tough and emotional time personally in the last 12 months, and he blew off steam recently when he won a sprint at the Tour de Romandie and celebrated with a two-finger salute to the world! He started to explain it with some old flannel about how British archers used to do that to the French at the Battle of Agincourt or something, but we knew exactly what the message was Mark. He copped a lot of criticism, was fined and deducted points, and was then withdrawn from the race by his team HTC-Columbia just when he was finding form and needed some race miles in his legs.

Sorry, I'm with Cav on this one and sympathised with him totally. Sometimes you have to lift the lid and let the steam out. We are not robots. How boring would sport be without characters like Cav? I txt him immediately to say heads up mate, and that he was a truly great rider. He seemed to appreciate that big time then, and again today when we nattered. He's in a humble subdued mood, the real Cav that not many people see. He can occasionally get a bit carried away with himself – mind you he has had more to get carried away with than most – but he soon comes back down to earth. This is a really big race for him though. It's been a troubled 2010 by his standards and his season will stand and fall by the Tour. I think he's ready to kick some arse again.

I've stopped tweeting for now by the way, and

I'm glad. For a while I really enjoyed it but it's dangerous territory when you're feeling vulnerable. You bash out a comment or a reaction to something in the heat of the moment and live to regret it, with people giving you grief for ages. It all ends in tears. Heaven knows what I would have put out into cyberspace today. Best left unsaid and let's try to rectify it a bit over the coming days.

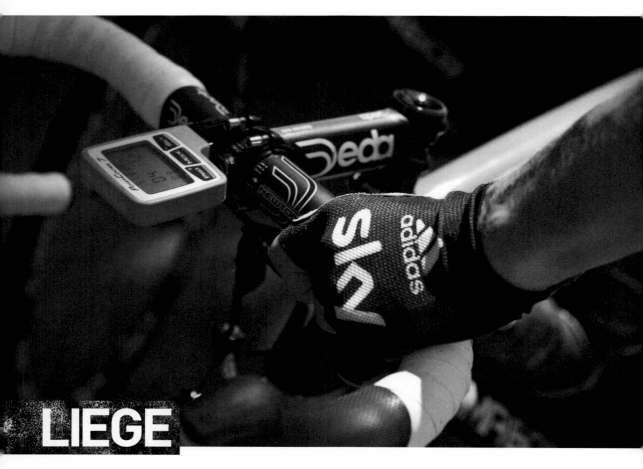

LIEGE

The Ramada Plaza, Quai St Léonard, Liège
Also in residence: on our own again

IT'S midnight and I'm still getting a pile of physiotherapy – ultrasound, interferential, massage – on my groin, which is bloody killing me. What a bitch of a day. Brussels–Spa had the look of a testing Ardennes classic and actually I was quite looking forward to it – it was not beyond the realms of possibility that I could have had a good day – but heavy rain falling on a hot road over the last third of the race, when we hit the short, sharp climbs, caused carnage on the descent of the Côte de Stockeu with, I reckon, at least a third of the peloton crashing. I've never seen anything like it. Very, very messy.

It was like ice. A complete lottery. Contador went down painfully, so did Lance, both Schlecks – I

think Andy ended up in the woods and was pictured looking for his bike apparently – poor old Christian Vande Velde is in hospital after yet another crash on his part, Dave Millar has broken some ribs or at least damaged them badly, George Hincapie went tumbling, and our own Michael Barry and Simon Gerrans as well. All sorts hit the deck, including me. I took a pretty nasty one, banged my knees and elbows and badly ripped a groin muscle which is a real worry this early in the Tour. I will put up with pain all day, but if a part of your body just isn't working mechanically you have no chance. My bike was in pieces so I 'borrowed' EBH's to try and chase up the road and rejoin the bunch.

After a bad crash the first thing you do is go into denial for a period of time and imagine you are still the same athlete and in the same condition as you were in the morning, but the truth is that

this evening, the same as for others out there, the reality is dawning. To be honest, just three days in and my Tour is already in the balance. I'm stuffed full of pain-killers and anti-inflammatories at the moment and we will make a call in the morning. I will be back on the physio's couch about 6.30 a.m. for another session.

I'm trying to be positive. I like to finish big races. This is my eighth Grand Tour – four Giro d'Italias and four Tour de France races – and I have finished them all except the 2007 Tour, when I was beginning to go really well in the final week only for my team Cofidis to get kicked out after Cristian Moreni tested positive. I admire people who stick with it and that is my intention, but I need that groin to improve overnight.

Enough of me. The real drama today was when yellow jersey Fabian Cancellara assumed the role

of the patron after the crashes. Sylvain Chavanel was out front on a break and that was fair enough, let him go, but those who were left in the bunch, with Fabian in control directing the pace from the front, slowed right down to allow us stragglers and victims to rejoin and a deal then appeared to be done whereby there would be no sprint finish and therefore no points would count towards the green jersey.

Patron is a term we use to acknowledge the 'boss' if you like of the peloton – the rider who, through his presence or weight of achievement, will organise the peloton to act together and show solidarity when there is something we are not happy about. In the past, when the Tour would really take the piss and organise two stages a day, or a 340 km stage, he would also determine when the peloton rode slow or at a steady tempo by way

of protest. I'm told that, on meaningless transition stages in the past, the patron would determine whether escapees who had no bearing on the GC were allowed to stay out and claim a valuable win for themselves and their team. By all accounts the greatest patron of them all was five-times Tour winner Bernard Hinault, who ruled with a rod of iron. Bernard is now helping run the Tour itself with ASO.

Humm . . . Very mixed feelings on this. On a selfish level, Fabian's intervention allowed me and others to rejoin the race and remain in contention after a shocking day in which my Tour prospects could have been killed off there and then. I supposed I shouldn't complain, but for me top-level bike racing is all about taking risks and riding your luck, almost every minute of every racing day, and if occasionally it all comes tumbling down for you

well that's tough. Stuff happens. We are back to my decision to chance my arm in the prologue again. Fortunes of war. That's how many Grand Tours and World Championships have been won from the year dot. That's how many youngsters get their first big break and start forging a reputation and a career.

It wasn't even as if the yellow jersey itself, which by tradition is protected when involved in a crash or chance accident, was involved in the carnage. He was up the road and safe, and had the potential of opening up a huge lead. These conventions are all very fine but it seems people are selective as to when they apply. Call me bitter and twisted but I don't remember any bugger waiting for me at the Giro back in May, when I held the leader's pink jersey after the prologue and then crashed badly the next day. Nobody showed the leader's jersey any courtesy then. Where were the racing traditions and

racing courtesies that day?

Yes, today was on a huge scale and I suppose the entire Tour as a spectacle was possibly at stake – the organisers would not want all the main GC contenders 5–10 minutes behind going into the Alps – but frankly, so what? That's racing. It's incidents like today that eventually become the stuff of legends. We shouldn't try to control and manipulate the racing. It you are unlucky and take a beating, take it like a man.

And what I can't agree with in any shape or form was the decision not to contest the finish after we had all brushed ourselves down and been allowed to re-gather with the bunch. Those who wanted to race should have been given the green light and those who just wanted to get home in one piece could decide at what pace they wanted to finish the day. The Tour de France lost integrity there, green

jersey contenders were denied a chance to do their thing, the sopping wet fans in Spa were offered nothing to cheer. Very poor. A bad day for the Tour de France and Pro-Tour cycling.

I'm not blaming Fabian, who is a very special rider I have been racing against for a decade or more. It's just that he was wearing the yellow jersey and, having avoided crashes himself, the onus fell on him to marshal things on the road. Remember he lost the yellow jersey by not chasing Chavanel, and no natural-born racer like Fabian would do that lightly. I have no doubt whatsoever that all the directeur sportifs were having their say to race organisers on race radio, and that the 'decision' to sit up and ride tempo was actually made as a 'collectif'. I suppose the natural patron these days is still Lance, but he was caught up in a bad crash himself and out of the equation. To an extent it

looks bad for Fabian, with his slowing of the race benefiting the Schlecks – his teammates – as they regained contact, but, in fairness, it benefited scores of other riders as well. It was just very messy and I feel for somebody like Thor Hushovd, who would have had big plans for a day like this and wasn't allowed to race. Strangest thing of all is that Chavanel, who was allowed to win, was also awarded green jersey points while nobody else was allowed to race. Pick the logic out of that if you will.

Plenty to talk about as ever, that's the way on Tour – you can't linger in any one place or on any one subject for long. When we woke up this morning ahead of this stage the sprint finish in Brussels was still playing itself over in many minds. Cav had a bad day at the office; I don't really know what happened there, I've only had a quick glance at the replay this evening, but he seemed to just

miss the final sharp right hand bend before the finishing straight. Most unlike him. Cav is normally inch-perfect on the sprint finishes with every bend and roundabout committed to memory. I wonder if that horrible Tour de Suisse crash – the last time he was in a bunch finish by my calculation – was playing on his mind at all. Probably not, he is totally fearless at the finish, but it would definitely be a factor with other riders who have got less bottle. Britain's Jeremy Hunt, riding his first Tour at 36, also went down on that bend. Hope he is ok, he's worked bloody hard over the years to earn this ride and it would be too cruel if it all ended on the second day.

PAVÉ

Hotel Saint Amand-les-Eaux
Also in residence: on our own again

THE much-anticipated pavé stage from Wanze to Arenberg lived up to all expectations. We've known for months that it would be carnage and that's exactly how it turned out, but it was also a cracking day on the bike and certainly revived my flagging spirits. I was up at dawn for more physio and to get my war wounds bathed, treated and bandaged – not feeling great, but a tad better than I expected. Certainly ok to go to the start line and give it a bash. At the start you could see everybody was on edge; it had the feel of a massive mountain stage, a day when riders could lose or gain large chunks of time. It's really early in the Tour for those sorts of decisive moves and nobody is quite sure of themselves.

I took it pretty gingerly to start with, not wanting to antagonise my groin, and we had Steve Cummings up in the break anyway, which was good. The pain-killers kicked in fairly quickly and gradually the groin muscles seemed to warm up and not complain too much, but I still entered the pavé well down from what I had originally intended – the theory being that you needed to be at the front of the bunch as you sprint into the pavé to avoid the carnage which normally follows behind, with the crashes and like.

It didn't work out like that at all, but for the first time in a good while lady luck shone on me a little today. In effect what happened is that as I maintained a good tempo and concentrated on keeping out of trouble, the front of the race simply came back to me and I moved up the field bit by bit without any dramas.

I have enjoyed riding the Paris–Roubaix race in the past and would like to have done it more often, but the big risk of an early season injury has often persuaded us to sit it out. You can't do it all these days, but one day I am going to make it a priority and give Paris–Roubaix the full monty. I love the crowd being so close – again, it's like the final stretch of a big mountain day, with riders feeding off their energy. Today was sunny and dry and very dusty despite the rain that hosed down yesterday, and as the peloton purrs through it kicks up a spectacular dust cloud. Back in April, when Paris–Roubaix is always held, it can be ankle deep in mud or the course can be covered in late snow and the riders who finish look like they have been mud wrestling. It's bike racing as you imagined as

a youngster and in fact not unlike those pick-up races when you race your mates around the park or estate. It's full on, great fun to ride and it must be brilliant to watch. I don't understand those who objected to a pavé stage in the Tour. If you want to crown the best bike rider in the world at the end of three weeks you have to have stages like this, the Tour shouldn't just be for the mountain goats, it's already stacked too heavily in their favour.

While other people were hitting the deck ahead of me – poor Frank Schleck had a shocker and put his left shoulder out on the second section, and Lance got held up by that and then had a major mechanical, puncture I think – I just kept plugging on, gradually managed to thread my way through pretty much untroubled and eventually found

myself in a high-quality chase group behind a six-man break which included our very own G, who was riding the race of his life.

My group came in a minute down and I even managed to put a few seconds into Alberto as I finished 8th. Very pleased with that – and a result that immediately sees me leap up to 14th in the GC. *Chapeaux* to Andy Schleck, what a great ride he put in today, just when many expected him to falter. He was pretty average in the prologue to say the least, losing 42 seconds to Contador which could ultimately cost him dear in GC, but he was magnificent today, riding in that lead group of six. Where did that come from? Of course he did have Spartacus – Fabian – to blast a path through for him and he would have been angry over Frank's crash but taken strength at the same time. Strange thing though, the potential for a crash today was almost

as great as yesterday on the run to Spa yet nobody seemed to have any qualms about attacking today.

Lance was a big loser on the day and, despite looking in great shape to me, nothing seems to be going his way at present. He came out with a classic Lancism at the finish though: 'Sometimes you are the hammer, sometimes you are the nail. Today I was the nail but I have been the hammer many times before.' He can't afford any more accidents though. I don't ever remember him falling off or getting punctures when he was winning his seven titles. That's nearly 150 days of Grand Tour riding on the bounce. And now two mishaps in two days. Perhaps his luck is running out.

MONTARGIS

Ibis Montargis, Place Victor Hugo
Also in residence: Team Milram

HAVE been in survival mode the last few days, looking after number one. Loved the pavé and the pictures in *L'Equipe* the following day were spectacular. Generally felt quite good but my wounds are still slow to heal and the groin still twanging as if it's on the verge of tearing altogether. Still got to take it very easy when I can. A lot of bruising is coming out from the Spa fall and I wish I felt better. I am not in great shape for this early in the race but I expect there are others in the peloton feeling exactly the same. We reach the mountains on Saturday so the two flat sprint stages – into Reims yesterday and Montargis today – were the last opportunity to take it relatively steady and to recover a little. So lots of massage, lots

of treatment, good eating and sleeping. It's been unbelievably hot these last few days; this is south of France heat right up here in the north. We can cope but it makes every day just that bit tougher.

The sprinters have taken over for the last couple of days and that means the trials and tribulations of Cav. He lost – fairly dismally – in Reims when he sat up at the end, which is pretty much a first for him as far as I can remember, so that was two sprints on the trot in which he didn't feature. And that was two sprint wins already for Alessandro Petacchi, who seems on good form and is clearly going to challenge for the green jersey.

People were beginning to scratch their heads and the press over-reacted a bit, sensing a major story or fall from grace. Was there something seriously wrong with Cav, either physically or mentally? I told them to wise up. Cav is pure class

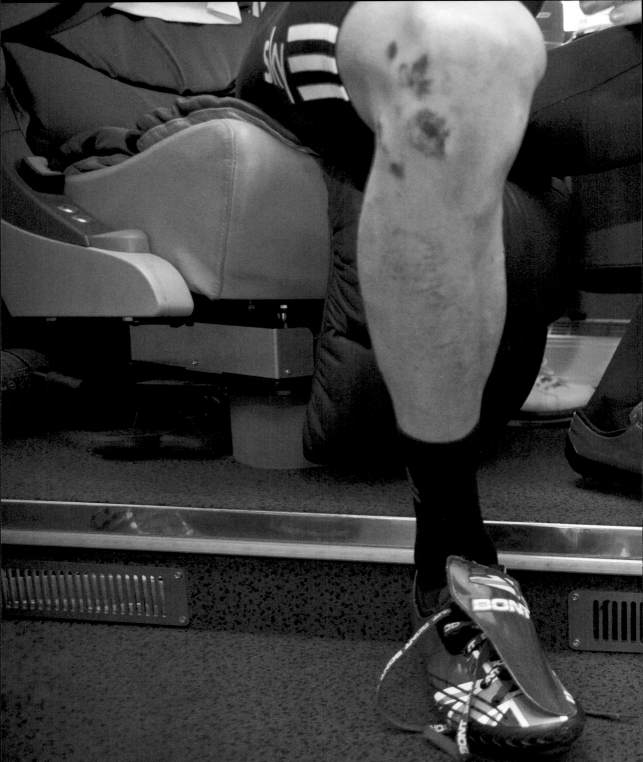

but he is just going through a trot where nothing good is happening. Ok, perhaps his confidence had taken a few dents, but we are talking the world's best sprinter here. It was a blip. I knew he would be back.

And today I was proved right as he took care of business in good style at Montargis after his Columbia train set him well. There were floods of tears afterwards from Cav, on TV, at the podium and behind the scenes, and you could see how much it means to him and also get a sense of how much pressure he is operating under. I am beginning to understand that much better and respect him even more for what he has done in the last two or three years. I feel under more pressure this year, being the team leader and the designated GC rider for Sky, but think what it must be like for Cav. Columbia's entire battle plan is to set Cav up for the sprint stages and if it doesn't happen for him he must feel absolutely devastated. He always talks about letting everybody down when that happens. Well he's back now big-time. Look out.

We claimed a couple of very useful third places in the sprints from EBH, which were good rides. EBH is an incredible talent – I can see him winning a major tour one day, yet he is strong in the one-day Classics, he can time-trial and he can mix it with the pure sprinters. It's all there in one package, it's a matter of putting it all together some day. But this year he has had two months out with an Achilles

problem and is not quite at the level he wants to be in this Tour. He was winning races for fun in 2009 but hasn't quite got that form at present. Getting involved with the likes of Cav, Petacchi, Julian Dean and Tyler Farrar in the sprints is a gutsy effort nonetheless.

THE ALPS

Hotel Saint Eusèbe, Le Pré au Bois
Also in residence: Footon-Servetto

LOST in France. This isn't a region that I know at all and, frankly, we could be anywhere. This is the calm before the storm – the Alps start tomorrow. For many that means the Tour proper starts then. They are wrong. It has been a savage first week, the heat has been freaky and the racing very hard. Everybody has been just melting and getting a bit frayed around the edges. Apparently we at Sky got through over 200 bottles of water on the road today. There is going to be a price to pay. A lot of really strong riders seem to be suffering already, which is always a good sign, and the racing is going to be erratic and unpredictable.

As I thought – I can't predict the weather but there are one or two certainties in sport – Cav is now on a roll and took today's stage in Gueugnon, beating Tyler Farrar into second place. Petacchi tucked in with a third place and, although I don't see Cav losing another sprint on this Tour now that he has got his act together, he is probably already too far behind to take that green jersey. Not getting on the scoreboard at all in those first two sprints was a disaster really; he's given everybody a big start. Petacchi, when he is in good shape, and Hushovd, are so consistent and are unlikely to just fade away. You never say never, and I suppose both of them could crash or get ill, but Cav has it all to do.

There are a lot of nerves again around the hotel tonight. Tomorrow is a big day for everybody and I'm hoping I might get a proper idea of how my form is. The groin is at about 85–90 per cent – it will have to do. The numbers on my test climbs near Girona

before the Tour were good – marginally better than last year actually – and putting aside the pain of the injuries this week I have actually felt quite strong on the flat. But form in the mountains is an art as well as a science: you can think you have got everything right and got the preparation bang on, and come the day you just don't have the legs.

There is a lot of speculation in the media that G could become the first British rider since Chris Boardman to take the yellow jersey tomorrow. He is currently second, just over 20 seconds behind Fabian Cancellara, and I suppose there is just a sniff, although he and the team are not getting too worked up about it. It doesn't do to try and get ahead of yourself on the Tour. On the assumption that the stage is not severe enough for the big hitters to make any major move, it would need Fabian to have a bad day in the mountains – he's

not a mountain goat but he can be very strong and determined when he wants to be – and for G to have an exceptional ride. There were signs on the Dauphiné Libéré recently that his climbing is improving big time. Let's just see.

Club Med, Avoriaz
Also in residence: BBOX Bouygues Telecom, Footon-Servetto, Garmin-Transitions, Katusha, Omega Pharma-Lotto, Milram

CROWDED house up here at Club Med! Morzine Avoriaz has become one of the Tour's great staging posts and this is our first rest day. I don't really like rest days and feel restless. Race-wise I am just about hanging in there and will know tomorrow, when we have the mountain day from hell to Saint-Jean-de-Maurienne, whether I have any chance of a

half decent finish in Paris. But for some the race is already effectively over. Lance crashed three times on the stage to Morzine today and is completely out of contention. Can't get my head around that yet but will try and think it through later.

Saturday's run from Tournus to Station des Rousses was much tougher than anybody expected. Everything is harder in this heat, when will it end? Those category two climbs felt much more like category ones to me, and early in a Tour they sometimes downgrade climbs anyway in anticipation of the really big stuff ahead. Saturday was a tough day. I did ok, moving up from 14th overall to 11th, finishing just under two minutes behind in the main chasing bunch behind Sylvain Chavanel, who went out on the break and really earned his yellow jersey this time, after being gifted it after the Spa stage. G's chances of a day in yellow

floundered on the final climb, the Lamoura. Bad luck, but G has had a brilliant first week.

Today's stage to Morzine Avoriaz was a killer. A massive storm and torrential rain last night shortly after the finish cleared the air for the start, back at Station des Rousses, but the baking sun was soon back and this was a stage that finished with two classic Alpine stages, the Col de la Ramaz and then the long haul up through Morzine and into Avoriaz.

But the fun started after just 6 km, in the gentle run out of Station des Rousses, when somebody lost concentration at the back as people were just cruising along and a bunch of riders went tumbling down. It was a costly crash. Lance was forced off into a ditch, Cadel Evans badly smacked his elbow and Simon Gerrans, having smashed his cheekbone during a crash on the pavé day, has now really hurt his arm. He is just back from the hospital now and

the news is bad: a clear broken arm. It was a bloody gutsy effort to get around yesterday but his Tour is over. It's a blow for Sky. Simon is a proven stage winner in the mountains if he gets in a break when the GC contenders are marking each other, and he had a big role to play for us. Things are not going our way.

Meanwhile Lance was going through all sorts of agonies; having recovered from that first crash he then suffered a second, nastier fall, at a roundabout in the approach to the Col de la Ramaz climb. The game was up after that and he was baulked a third time in the final stage by an Euskatel rider. He eventually finished a distant 61st, nearly 12 minutes behind stage winner Andy Schleck. He has no chance now. His career as a competitive rider in the Tour de France is over. Just watching some of the footage now and his face after the second crash

said it all, he knew it was finally over.

Just don't know what to say or think. I am a massive Lance fan and never thought it would end like this for him. He looks so strong to me but you just can't contend with the kind of bad luck he has experienced in the first week or so. Although he dominated for those seven years – when I can remember him having two mishaps at the most, both in 2003 – like I say, the Tour always has the last word. Wonder how he will approach it now? We still have two weeks to go. Some reckon he will find a way of quitting in a few days, but that's not his style; he will see it out and will probably try for a stage win in the Pyrenees. I still maintain he's basically in good form but has just suffered from having no luck. It takes ages to get into that kind of shape, why waste it?

I didn't enjoy today much. The final sections of the long drag up to Avoriaz were very hard and I lost about 1 min. 30 to the chase group with Contador and Evans in it. I am mystified because I felt very easy on the first climb – the Col de la Ramaz – and was coping pretty well for most of the main last climb. But I reached a point at about 1400 m when I immediately began to suffer. Was it the heat or altitude, or have I got my training wrong? Thomas Lofkvist, who is going well, did a great job sticking with me and seeing me home to limit my losses, but it's a worry. I am now 19th in GC, 2 min. 44 secs behind. We are in the last-chance saloon in terms of trying to make a race of it this year.

I've just been down into Morzine proper to meet the British press and it's hard trying to put a positive spin on things when, deep down, I am pretty concerned myself. I try my best though. I told them – and actually I believe it – that if I was only

2 min. 45 off the pace in Paris that would mean I would be on the podium, which would be a major result and everybody would be happy. That's not such a daft statement as it sounds. But that is assuming I begin to fire on all four cylinders in the mountains like I did last year.

I found the press session quite an ordeal, although I like to think I get on with most of the press guys pretty well. There is so much expectation to do well this year, but you can never just order up success on the Tour and, of course, you have to try and keep up a positive front. The one thing you are never forgiven for in sport is throwing in the towel. What would be nice though is if I could be absolutely straight with the guys and say 'Look, we've had some good moments, but for me things aren't going as smoothly as we had hoped. It's been a bloody hard Tour already – the pace has been manic, I got

badly banged around on the Spa stage, it's bloody hot even by Tour de France standards and I am much more fatigued at this stage than I was last year. We are learning a stack of lessons every day. I will never give up and I live in hope of riding myself into real form and making an impact in the second half of the Tour. That sometimes happens. But you know how it is. Sometimes it just doesn't happen for you in this sport.'

That's what I'm thinking but publicly I am trying to be more upbeat. I would like to crack a few jokes too, but when the foreign press are there as well as the Brits they don't always get my sense of humour and I say stuff that gets me into trouble. It's not worth the hassle.

Being in Morzine again reminds me of my first Tour in 2006, when the epic Floyd Landis escape finished here and he won the stage by miles, after

'cracking' the previous day on the final climb when he seemed dead to the world. We then had a rest day here and I don't think I have ever felt so tired in my life. None of us quite knew what to make of the Landis ride. You wanted to believe it because it was dramatic and exciting but ... Anyway, a few days later it all kicked off when Landis was found to be positive for testosterone on that stage and stripped of the Tour title. Amazing to think that entire story is still running around, with Landis recently admitting his guilt after denying it for four years in court – and spending a lot of money donated by his fans in denying it. And now he is coming out with scatter-gun accusations concerning loads of his former colleagues. It has become very messy indeed.

What a totally mad and confusing Tour that 2006 race was for a debutant. The Départ in Strasbourg was dominated by the Operation Puerto revelations and huge names like Jan Ullrich and Ivan Basso – and others – being withdrawn as their teams asked them for explanations as to what had been going on down in Spain. Then we finished with the Landis nonsense. My simple aim at the time was to do my bit for my team – Cofidis – and to get around, tick that box which says I had finished a Tour de France and then just get out of that mad often drug-fuelled world. I am a glass half-full person but I was very disillusioned and completely spent at the end of the 2006 Tour de France. I had no intention of returning, to be honest.

ON THE BUS

THE TEAM BUS takes on a massive importance when you are on tour; it's your home from home, your refuge if you like. On a bad day just getting to the bus is a target in itself. It is the one place of permanence in a revolving door of a month in which you are either checking in, checking out or spending six hours a day on the move at speed on your bike. The bus is where you stop the world for an hour or two and get yourself together, either before or after a race. I still find it fascinating to sit behind those darkened windows watching the world go by. Be warned. We can see out perfectly but you can't look in on us, the ideal scenario as far as I am concerned.

The madness of it all still gets me every time on the Tour. The bus nudges its way through the throng as we make our way to our allotted parking area. The team buses seem to act as a magnet to

fans and supporters, who gather almost from the moment we pull up about an hour or 90 minutes before the race starts. Often there isn't a huge amount to see, although there is always a little ruffle of excitement when the mechanics set our bikes out on their stands and one or two of us will normally pop out to say a hello and acknowledge the fans. The press, of course, will also be hanging around outside, waiting for a 'quick word' with whoever emerges. DaveB normally obliges, and I will if I can. Mind you, on the morning of a big stage I can't really see the point of saying too much – you can be left with egg on your face six hours later, so much can change – but sometimes they want to talk about more general themes or preview a particular stage a few days down the road.

In the old days, when I started riding the Tour – what am I talking about, that was only four

years ago in 2006 – I would often wander into the Tour village for 20 minutes, where all the small breakfast kiosks and sponsors' stands are set up. It seemed like the thing to do; it was certainly what all the riders seemed to do in the old books and films. Of course nobody knew me from Adam then, so it was nice and relaxing. I would wander over to the Crédit Lyonnais tent, grab a café noir and a muffin and settle down for 10 minutes to read the English papers, which they seemed to have flown in that year. Either that or I would have a casual chat with the British scribes, normally nothing to do with cycling. It was pretty relaxing and I can remember Dave Millar and G joining us on a few occasions. It has changed very quickly since then though. It all seems a bit frantic in the village now – you get pulled over for autographs and photos or another set of interviews – and more and more I have found

that I value every minute back in the bus. So much so that I leave it as late as possible now to head out to sign on before the start of the race. I am always the last to leave the bus now, and when the others are gone I get the coach driver Gwilym Evans to turn the sound up and blast out two or three of my favourite numbers on top volume. After that I am good to go.

Gwilym is not only the driver, he is in charge of the coach and has been a good addition to the Sky Team. Being Welsh he is a huge rugby fan and, living near Northampton, Saints are his club, but he loves sport generally. He worked for years in the world of Formula 1 so has had plenty of experience of working with sportsmen under extreme stress and seems to like the way we go about our work. He was working with Simtec the day Roland Ratzenberger was killed at Imola in 1994 and is one

of the last people to have a long conversation with Ayrton Senna who died the next day. Apparently the Simtec mechanics and Gwilym were in the garage around midnight after Ratzenberger's dreadful death and had just made the decision to 'build' a car overnight so their second driver could compete. Senna apparently called in and spent the best part of half an hour offering his condolences and support for the team. A few hours later, of course, he was dead himself.

Our coach on this Tour was state-of-the-art, although not quite so space-age as some reports made out. DaveB loves talking things up a little because it keeps the opposition guessing as to what might be. It's like our track programme and our famous 'Secret Squirrel' club, headed by Chris Boardman, looking into technological innovations. Yes, they are always on the case and have made some very good contributions to the cause, but if you build up a little mystery about it opposition imaginations can run wild and they can be left thinking they definitely have inferior bikes and kit, which is rarely the case. At the top level now there is rarely much of a difference to talk about.

I suppose the first thing you notice about the Sky Bus is the blue strobe light on the roof, which helps guide us home in the crowded parking area at the end of the day, and the big satellite dish on the roof. The satellite dish does of course mean we can get TV coverage from around the world, and that our backroom staff can record footage from the day and have it available for us to watch soon after the stage. With the satellite in place communciations are superb – internet, wifi and Skype. We have everything. On the morning of a stage DaveB and the directeur sportif will roll down one of those mobile screens and do a Powerpoint presentation. It won't be a huge production, short sharp and succinct. We will have a quick resumé of what our targets are for the day and everyone will be made aware of what their roles are and the options should it not all work out. DaveB might illustrate it with a diagram or two, or, if we are looking at something specific like a sprint lead-out,

Dave or one of the DSs might have some footage of our most recent lead-outs to discuss. We all had our allocated seats and, as team leader, mine is nice and handy, just across from the steps so I can collapse into it at the end of a stage. I used to sit there, my immediate post-race recovery drink and a bowl of rice would be brought to me, and I would eventually strip off and shower and get into some different gear, maybe get a massage under way if we have a long transfer.

One of the first things to do getting back to the bus is always to phone Cath to reassure her I am ok, especially if it has been a tough one or there has been a rash of accidents. I'm a family man and it can be hard on the road sometimes but generally I cope pretty well. I go into my race bubble and the bottom line is that I am living my dream, doing exactly what I dreamed of doing years ago and getting well rewarded for the honour. And it's not forever. I still get masses of quality time at home with my wife and children. It's work, taking care of business.

If I'm absolutely honest I don't think we quite got it right on the Sky Bus on the Tour this year, through nobody's fault. Don't get me wrong, it could hardly have been any more comfortable and better appointed, but there were times when it lacked a little soul. What happens when you are sitting in extreme comfort in your specially designed chair and you have got your earphones and iPod, and your wifi and your laptop? Well, unless you are careful, what happens is that you can go into your shell and start inhabiting your own world and stop relating to other people. I definitely felt that starting to happen on some occasions on this Tour and was guilty of withdrawing. Of course there is no harm wanting your occasional quiet moments on the bus, especially as you recover on the way to the next hotel each evening after a brutal stage – that is completely natural. But to me the team bus also serves a big role as the place where you come together as a team, when a lot can be achieved through good old-fashioned banter and mixing. What I increasingly found was that in the morning,

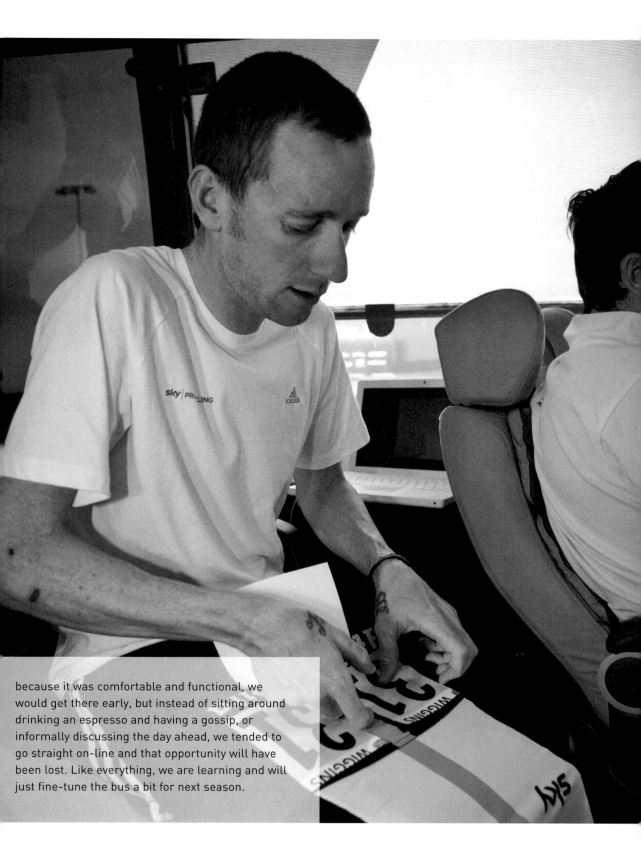

because it was comfortable and functional, we would get there early, but instead of sitting around drinking an espresso and having a gossip, or informally discussing the day ahead, we tended to go straight on-line and that opportunity will have been lost. Like everything, we are learning and will just fine-tune the bus a bit for next season.

DAYS OFF

DAYS off, I hate them really. The Tour is a three-week race that needs to be ridden and two days off at the end of the first week and second week just get in the way. No matter how well or badly you are going the body gets into a rhythm. Up, breakfast massage, an hour on the bus to the start, five or six hours on the bike, bus, hotel massage, food, sleep. It knows what's going on. And then suddenly you throw a spanner in the works. If you truly treated a 'Day off' as just that, and slept late and mooched around the hotel swimming pool all day, or lounged around an inviting looking cafe drinking coffee, you would never be able to get up the next morning and swing your leg over the bike. The body would stiffen up and all the muscles begin to harden and get sore.

What is it they say about banging your head against a brick wall? It only hurts when you stop.

Well there is definitely a bit of that with the Tour de France. Or rather, it hurts even more when you stop. By the middle of the race your body is an engine that is working flat out, revving high. You fill it with fuel every day – about 5000–6000 calories of food, sometimes more on a big mountain day – and off you go. A day off can be like suddenly stalling the engine. You splutter to a halt and then suddenly you have to start all over again for the next couple of days, going through the gears and getting back to whatever your peak performance is that year. Nowadays it's pretty accepted practice that you go out for a ride on your rest day, it's what your body craves and is telling you to do. And not just a gentle spin. The perceived wisdom now is two or three hours' pretty hard labour, with at least one decent climb to work up a sweat. Which, when you think about it, is self-defeating. And that's my point. If all

the riders are out and about on their bikes for two or three hours on their rest day, we might as well be racing a four- or five-hour stage. The rest of the time will be hanging around basically and filling in time. There is usually a press conference to do in the afternoon or evening, so that hangs over you, and the day can definitely drag. There is so much of the Tour still to ride and on rest days the temptation is to think ahead and to brood about what's coming up. Much better to be busy and keep chipping away day by day. Talking around the peloton, I think my view is pretty widely shared. I suspect modern-day rest days are more for the race organisation, the sponsors and the media than for the riders. For the media, they probably do need a day every week or so to take stock and dash around doing a load of interviews on the story of the Tour. And the sponsors definitely need to be in the same place

for a couple of nights to set up their camps, invite some valued guests over and do a corporate day. I suppose there is also an argument which says the TV viewer probably wants the occasional rest. All I know is that I can't ever remember having a good day on the Tour the day after the rest day, and that was certainly the case this year after the first rest day in Morzine.

LANCE ARMSTRONG

LANCE Armstrong divides the cycling world but, love him or loathe him, believer or disbeliever, all of us in the peloton are definitely in his debt. There is no way I would be earning the money I am today in a British team with Tour de France aspirations without Lance's overall influence on the sport. An English-speaking megastar with charisma and an amazing story to tell, he has opened the sport up to a much wider audience and helped take cycling around the world. Lance Armstrong has changed the sport of cycling.

After the Festina affair in 1998 and the drug mayhem that followed, there was every possibility that professional cycling would hit the rails as a sport, at least as a sport with a worldwide profile outside of north-west Europe. Public opinion was going heavily against the sport but Lance's fight for life and fitness after contracting and then

overcoming cancer gave professional road cycling a 'good news' story to get us back on the sports pages for the right reasons. Just what the doctor ordered in fact. Looking back, he probably became the biggest sports story in the world for a number of years, he raised cycling's profile tenfold and he got sponsors and the money men back on board.

He attracted the general sporting public, who had shown a growing interest in the sport during the 1980s, when TV coverage boomed, to again take an interest in the Tour de France. There is no doubt in my mind that, without Lance Armstrong, the Tour was in serious trouble, but he provided the interest and focus on the race again. I am also convinced that 'debt' they owe to Armstrong is one of the reasons the French press, and often the public, took against him. For a while there he bailed the Tour de France out and, in the short term, became almost bigger than the Tour. There have been serial winners in the past – Jacques Anquetil won five in quick succession, so did Bernard Hinault and Eddy Merckx, so did Miguel Indurain. There was an American, English-speaking champion in Greg Lemond as well, just before Lance started out, and he seemed popular enough. But none of them received the waves of criticism Lance endured. And, let's be honest, the subject of drugs and the suggestion that one or two great champions during the Tour's long history might have resorted to using drugs is not exactly a novel idea. It was almost part of the folklore. What the French media and public really hated was the idea that one man from Texas was so scientific in his approach to winning the Tour every year and, with the help of his hand-picked team, seemed to batter the race and his opponents into submission. I suppose he took the romance out of the Tour.

As I sit and write this the FDA (Food and Drug Administration) in the USA are looking into the Floyd Landis allegations concerning Lance when they rode together at US Postal. Who knows what will come out of that and if their top agent, Jeff Novitzky, will find a case that needs answering? All I can do at this stage is tell you about the Lance Armstrong I have ridden with on the last couple on Tours.

Lance moves in another orbit really, it's difficult to get a handle on him. This is a guy who has nudging 3 million Twitter followers. This is a bloke who can tweet one night that he might go for a short training ride in the rain in Glasgow the next morning and turn up before breakfast to find 400 weekend warriors to accompany him. American presidents queue to be pictured with him and, when France's President Sarkozy was on hand at the summit finish at the Tourmalet this year, it was Lance he wanted to meet first, only then followed by stage winner Andy Schleck and the yellow jersey Alberto Contador, who had to take their place in the line. He's got an aura about him, no question, you can sense it. You know when Lance has entered the room even before you see him, and you always know exactly where he is in the bunch without

necessarily seeing him.

During the last two years I have got to know the man, not the legend, just a little better, through riding with him and enjoying some short but revealing chats. Before then I didn't know him any better than any cycling fan on the street.

To start with I was pretty much in awe of him. He was this world figure who commanded his team like a general and achieved near miracles every July. He appeared flawless and unbeatable. He always arrived in perfect shape – his main rival Jan Ullrich was always half a stone or more overweight – he never seemed to crack in the mountains and he always won the decisive time-trial. He had great ability right across the board, a bunch sprint is just about the only thing he can't do. He always prevailed, even when his personal life was getting complicated. He was like something from a Hollywood movie really, and of course there have been plans over the years to do just that: make the film.

My impressions before I actually spoke to him were of a very tough cookie who you wouldn't want to cross, a driven individual who lived only for the Tour. Knowing him better now I realise I was only partly right. He certainly lives for the Tour and there is never any doubt who the 'boss' is when he is around, but there is another dimension as well.

I've always found Lance friendly and helpful. We started on nodding terms at the Tour of Murcia in 2009 and by the Tour that year we would always stop for a chat. He knew all about my track career, not just the general stuff and the medals but the actual performances and times I had put in and, being a bike nut, was fascinated by those trying to make the crossover from track to road racing. He is interested in everything and anything to do with bike riding, he will have a go at anything and he's got an eye for the riders with raw talent coming through. He knows who's got what it takes.

On the first big climb of the 2009 Tour, from Barcelona up to Arcalis in Andorra, he suddenly rode up to me at the bottom of the climb and said: 'This is a good climb for you Wiggo, long and steady, go well.' It was a big moment for him as well, and he must have been keyed up, so I was impressed and a little dumbfounded that he had thought to ride up with a word of encouragement for me. Later in the Tour, right at the end of stage 17 from Bourg Saint Maurice to Le Grand Bornand, he put a minute into me at the end of the stage which we had ridden together and came up to me at the end and apologised! It was somehow as if we were getting through the Tour together and he felt he might have broken that bond. Of course he hadn't. He did what the situation demanded. He was riding strong and it was time for him to disappear up the road.

Lance didn't get the credit he deserved for that third place in 2009. Considering he hadn't ridden since 2005, had smashed his collarbone in the spring and was chronically short of race training, it was a fine effort. I didn't think he looked in incredible shape at the start in Monte Carlo but he made himself very competitive by his mental strength and the force of his personality to get Astana largely riding for him and not Alberto. That was a very strange, occasionally amusing situation to observe from the sidelines, but it was always going to be the case. Lance has to be the leader of any team he rides in. He is a natural racer. On that windy day from Marseille to La Grande Motte in stage 3 he knew exactly the potential for a split and rode hard at the front all day while others – like myself and Alberto Contador to name just two – took our eyes off the ball a bit and got caught in the middle of the bunch when the split came at that sharp right hand bend. He put 40 seconds into us that day simply with his racing nous. This year again I have found no side in him at all, despite the fact that everything was suddenly happening to him and almost nothing of it good. He suddenly had seven years of stored up bad luck thrown at him in the first week. He handled it really well in my opinion. Lance didn't throw the toys out of the pram, he didn't whinge, he just got on with the business of riding every day in the Tour de France. His basic fitness was pretty good, he was definitely capable of a top five without all the rubbish that

happened to him. I'm biased and perhaps not objective as some people would like when it comes to Lance. I wasn't battered senseless by him and his team during the glory years between 1999 and 2005. I was safely at home watching on the TV. I didn't have to take defeat on the chin on a daily basis or indulge in verbal jousting matches. He is very articulate and it's almost impossible to get the last word with him. I have been treated to the mellower post-2005 Lance.

Frankly, it has been an unexpected bonus to ride the Tour twice with him and, even on those two occasions in the autumn of his career, I could sense what an incredible competitor and once-in-a-generation athlete he was and is. During his run of seven consecutive years he was completely unstoppable. He must have been a complete nightmare to ride against, very demoralising.

That 'stare' he has sometimes when he is on the limit going up a climb is usually pretty scary. He sort of goes in on himself, blotting out the real world of a 10 per cent climb over 20 km in hot sunshine and the endless pain and suffering that goes with it. I suppose it's a trance of sorts, I sometimes wish I could emulate it.

He built his team around him, trained only for the Tour and made winning the Tour an art form. Having overcome cancer he was willing to drive himself harder and suffer more than anybody else. Looking on from the outside, the two things that shone through every time were, first, that he wanted it much more than any other rider and, second, he was simply a better all-round rider than anybody else of his era.

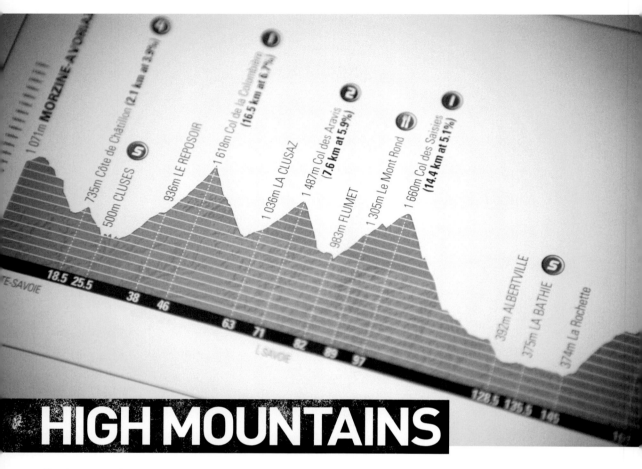

The profile chart shows (left to right): 1 071m MORZINE-AVORIAZ · 735m Côte de Châtillon (2.1 km at 3.9%) · 500m CLUSES · 936m LE REPOSOIR · 1 618m Col de la Colombière (16.5 km at 6.7%) · 1 036m LA CLUSAZ · 1 487m Col des Aravis (7.6 km at 5.9%) · 983m FLUMET · 1 305m Le Mont Rond · 1 660m Col des Saisies (14.4 km at 5.1%) · 392m ALBERTVILLE · 375m LA BATHIE · 374m La Rochette

HIGH MOUNTAINS

Hotel Astoria, Place des thermes, Aix-les-Bains
Also in residence: Cofidis

SO now we know. It's not going to happen for me this year, I'm not in the shape to compete for the 2010 Tour de France and somewhere along the line we have got it wrong. It's bloody disappointing, frustrating, upsetting – all of that – but also it's a weight off my shoulders. I don't have to go through the motions of pretending to still be a podium candidate. I can tell people how it is and try to enjoy the rest of the race for what it is. I've given it everything but my top-end climbing just isn't there this summer, and without that you can't compete in the Tour de France.

Feeling a bit sorry for myself if I am honest. I've let everybody down, but there is a long way to go so got to snap myself out of that. We can still salvage a few bit and pieces from this Tour.

Today was always going to be a big test, a huge mountain stage from Morzine to Saint-Jean-de-Maurienne, over the Colombière, the Col des Aravis and then the mighty Col de la Madeleine, which climbs for nearly 26 km at an average gradient of over 6 per cent, with a couple of really nasty sections in the second half: 66 km of climbing, the most mountainous day of the Tour. The moment of truth. The sun was still beating down and the day after a rest day can be very tricky. Well, that's how I find it anyway. I hate the interruption to routine and momentum, I much prefer just to keep pressing on. My game plan was pretty simple, to somehow stay in touch and then use the 30 km descent to reduce my losses, but in the end I finished 4 min. 45 secs behind the winner Sandy Casar and am now 16th overall, 7 min. 18 behind Andy Schleck, who has

taken over the yellow jersey.

I didn't feel brilliant at any stage but it wasn't until the final climb – the Madeleine – that I got dropped from the elite group who were chasing the four-man break which included Anthony Charteau and Casar. I just couldn't go with Andy Schleck, Contador and Samuel Sanchez and the others, and had to settle for survival and getting home as best I could. I was in good company, mind, as a lot of quality riders were hitting the same wall – Cadel, although in fairness he was riding with a broken elbow, Carlos Sastre, Michael Rogers, Chris Horner, Nicolas Roche and Ryder Hesjedal, with Andreas Kloden and Alexandre Vinokourov only just up the road.

Again it was when I got over 1400–1450 metres that I hit trouble – the Madeleine is a whopping 2000 m at the summit – which is a bit confusing and worrying. I have raced at altitude this year – completed the Giro and did all the big climbs on that – and done day recces on selected climbs, but the one thing I haven't done and have never really done is a prolonged training camp at altitude. Living and training there for a fortnight or more. Talking to some of the boys it seems that, almost to a man, they have done big blocks of altitude training specifically for the Tour this year. I wonder if we are missing a trick here. Also, looking around, nobody who rode the Giro this year seems to be tearing up trees – Basso and Sastre especially, although Cadel was going well until his crash. You had to go deep in the Giro this year, even just to get around, and I think we are seeing the consequences of that as well. We will have plenty to chew over when we review the race but one thing that seems clear to me is that I need to get to grips with altitude

training, and if we go that route it's probably impossible logistically to race the Giro as well.

It's probably not that simple though. Somebody mentioned that it might be 'second album syndrome', which is a phrase I find useful. You know how it is, you have a great and unexpected success but how do you follow it up? How do you top what might just be the very best you ever achieve in your career? Do you stick to what brought you that success or do you try to build on it and branch out in other directions, and push your abilities further? Hopefully there is a platinum album waiting down the line somewhere.

Have got to try and refocus now. A top-ten position is not totally out of the question if I come good in the Pyrenees, but if I maintain this form I will finish 20-something. It would be nice if we could start picking up a stage or two and I have got

my eye on the final time-trial, the day before Paris, although it's too early to start thinking seriously about that. I've got to reach Bordeaux first.

There were emotional pictures of Cadel on the TV just now, collapsing into the arms of his colleague Mauro Santambrogio at the end of the stage and crying his eyes out. He eventually came in just over 8 minutes behind Casar. I know exactly how Cadel must feel. He must have been in a lot of pain and wearing the yellow jersey and defending it is a big emotional job as well. He buried himself and had nothing left at the end. It was a gutsy effort but he knows his chances of winning the Tour ended today as well. It can be very tough out there.

TEAM MECHANICS

THEY never, I mean absolutely never, get a mention so let's rectify that right now. Step forward the Team Sky mechanics – Rajen Murugayan, Filip Tisma, Igor Turk, Diego Costa, Frederik Moon, David Fernandez, Alan Williams, Kenneth van de Welle – who basically keep the show on the road. They set up a mobile workshop out the back of everywhere we stop and keep the nine riders' bikes in perfect working order for three weeks. They set the bikes and spares up, hose them down at the end of every day, repair them when damaged, anticipate when we want to change the tyres and set up, check every moving part endlessly and generally perform wonders, almost always against the clock, because time waits for no man when you are on the road. You can hear them tinkering away when you turn in every night and you often wake to the noise of them working away, cursing in the

early morning and packing up outside. Being the way of the world we shout at them and whinge if anything goes wrong – which is very rarely – but forget to praise them for their hard work and professionalism. I can't imagine they earn a fortune but these are guys who are there mainly for the love of the sport and the love of the beautiful bikes they prepare and cherish. To watch them beavering away is to observe real craftsmen at work. Every team on the Pro-Tour has them but ours at Team Sky are among the best. There you go guys!

CAV

INTELLIGENT – scarily intelligent in a non-academic way – honest, courageous, intuitive, fiery and very sensitive. Too sensitive sometimes perhaps. Who am I talking about? Mark Cavendish of course who I have known and admired for most of his career on the track and on the road. Cav fascinates me like few other riders in that he lives in a very confrontational world, with the tag of being the world's fastest bike rider. Those guys – Cav, Robbie McKewen, Alessandro Petacchi, Tyler Farrar – are like 100 metre sprinters and heavyweight boxing champions in that they can never betray a moment's weakness or vulnerability. That's why some of them tend to mouth off so much! You can't really admit to something being wrong in your technique or basic talent, even when you lose or are struggling with your form, or else the others will pounce on it.

There is that Muhammad Ali sort of swagger – you have to rout the opposition verbally and mentally as well as physically. As a person in everyday life you might be nothing like that, but when you go to work you have to adopt that kind of persona if you are a sprinter.

From what I have seen, at the basic level, they all get on well enough given the chance. Early in the day you will sometimes catch them having a natter in the peloton, but in the last hour of a sprint day they morph into different people altogether and go to war with each other – there is no other way of describing it. The confrontations can get very physical, personal and dangerous.

The sprinters live in another world from the rest of us. For us non-sprinters the main battle is always with the race and the terrain, the rain and the heat. I will chat with almost any of my rivals when it's quiet or at the start of the day, and then we will go in on ourselves and fight our own battles for the day. We race against each other, yes, and certainly when you see Alberto and Andy go at it in the mountains you are witnessing a proper duel, but ultimately the war is with the course – the Tourmalet, Alpe d'Huez, the Col de la Madeleine. Afterwards there is rarely any attitude or bad feeling – we have done our best

on the day and the results are there in black and white to see who was the best. We very rarely lose by inches like the sprinters.

So I have tons of respect for the tough world the sprinters operate in. Cav is undoubtedly the King at present. I am biased because I am British and he's a mate, but to my mind he is the fastest sprinter the Tour de France has ever seen. I refuse to believe there has been anybody who can match his top-end speed in the last 275–300 metres on a flattish finish. Amazing, it takes your breath away. Twice now he has won on the Champs Elysées with bursts beyond any rider I have known. He is fast becoming a legend of the sport.

The British sporting public don't even begin to appreciate him yet. Between July 2008 and July 2010 he won 15 Tour de France stages. That is absolutely phenomenal, the sport has never seen anything like that in terms of consistency and the ease with which he often pulls those victories off. More often than not, Cav is slowing down or soft pedalling over the line to save himself for the next sprint, and the one after that. If he stays fit and healthy I can see him winning another 20 Tour stages at least, and in terms of his world-wide reputation he will finish his career right up there with the likes of Eddy Merckx and Lance Armstrong. That's the measure of the man.

He will win the green jersey one day. His climbing and all-round ability is improving every year so he is beginning to get around the big Grand Tours with a bit more in the tank and he will never lose that ability to take stages. And he must stand every chance at the 2012 Olympics. That's always a difficult race to call but I think we can safely assume it will be a sprint finish. He can freestyle the finish if he has to, but the challenge for Great Britain will be to develop enough quality riders to provide him with a lead-out train of the quality he gets at HTC-Columbia.

Never underestimate Cav's intelligence and the way he prepares for races. In the final stages he races by instinct, but only after all the information about the finish and those around him has been fed

into that computer of a brain. When the media catch him straight after a finish, and he's completely knackered and emotional, it can't be easy to give a coherent and rational explanation as to what has just gone on, but I have sat down with him later in the evening after a win and he will tell you in incredible detail exactly what happened, when and why he reacted as he did. It's all there. Everything has been digested and analysed. He has instant recall on all his finishes, wins and losses.

He is sensitive and can take things to heart – comments in the press he disagrees with or thinks are just plain inaccurate and ill-informed. But that comes from being a very honest character. Nobody is a harsher critic of his own riding than Cav himself. He gets angry with himself when he is not in shape and form, and takes steps to rectify that immediately. He doesn't have to be told when extra work needs to be done. He always puts his hand up when he has let his team down but, equally, he will not hesitate to tell them, or the back-up staff, when they have not delivered properly or have overlooked something. If people can't deal with that approach, that is their problem not his. It's the right approach if you want to win and achieve great things.

We have shared some great moments and, of course, one crushing disappointment at the Beijing Olympics. The high point was probably when we won the World Madison title together in Manchester in 2008. We were strong favourites – if you can ever be favourite in a race like the Madison – and everybody was trying to mark us out of the race, but we were both in brilliant form and somehow we gave them the slip and brought it home. The crowd went nuts; it was like a football crowd every time we attacked, I've never heard such an atmosphere in the velodrome. A really happy day. That night, though, there was another example of why Cav is so successful. After three World Championship golds in a week – I had won the Individual Pursuit and GB had won the Team Pursuit – we all set off to town for liquid refreshment and a big Saturday night out. Cav came along for the crack but he didn't touch a

drop; he had a big race on the Monday and nothing was going to divert him from that. He is a model professional and I can see why he quickly became the team leader at HTC-Columbia.

It was that win in Manchester that convinced us we could go for the exact same treble in Beijing, but we were wrong. Heading towards Beijing I was laid up with a bad virus and I wasn't as strong as five months earlier. Also, there were more qualifying rounds in the Pursuit events and when I reached the Madison on the final day I was really tired and it just didn't happen for us. Cav had cut short his Tour de France – he had won four stages while there! – to concentrate on the Olympics and it was a bitter blow that the Madison went pear-shaped, the one real failure in an amazing Track Championship for the Brits. We had a few words and things were cool for a bit, but we are absolutely fine now and his Olympic moment will come.

Cav has been a trail-blazer in many ways. He's still only 25 but has achieved so much, a Brit who is probably second only to Contador as a world-wide cycling star now that Lance is bowing out. That's pretty elite territory and I suspect it can't have been easy marrying that with a fair few personal issues. To my mind, he manages brilliantly, but the first half of 2010 was undoubtedly a big low with his health problems, a lack of form at times, a really nasty crash at the Tour de Suisse and a number of other issues in the background. He arrived at the Tour with the eyes of the world looking at him, many waiting for him to fail. The pressure must have been immense but, as usual, he delivered in spades.

BASTILLE DAY

Hotel Carina, Le Pavillion, Gap
Also in residence: Team Milram

THE TOUR finally took its foot off the pedal today, and not before time after a pretty insane first week or so. Just by way of self-preservation we had to have a sensible day and many of the riders were in pieces after battling through the mountains for three days. Not that today was a doddle by any means. The Col de Laffrey was a category one climb and has been on the Tour since 1905, and the Col du Noyer was steady and high though thankfully not too steep.

The Bastille Day crowd wanted to see us racing flat out but the peloton, except for the six-man break, were having none of it and were looking for an easy day. Well – as easy as you can get in this heat. No patron needed on this occasion, it was just a collective decision. Mike Rogers at HTC-Columbia has just tweeted to say that when we were skirting around Grenoble at lunchtime he looked down at his small onboard computer and it showed 46°C on the road. It's absolutely ridiculous to be riding in that temperature, and the real heat of the day doesn't really build up until mid afternoon.

Luckily, as we swept down into Gap, a nice breeze did kick up, but although the holiday makers may have lapped it all up, riding conditions were far from pleasant. Overheating is a real problem and you spend a lot of time simply remembering to take liquids on board and trying to keep your core temperature down. One old trick a few of the team use is to cut up some ladies stockings or tights, cram them with ice and then make a sausage around the back of your neck to keep you cool and to keep the sun off. Needs must, really.

As for the race up the front, Portugal's Sergio Paulinho, who won an Olympic silver medal in 2004, seemed to thrive in the conditions and made his own break from the escape with about 14 km to go, chased by Vasil Kiryienka from Belarus. They had a ding-dong battle down the finishing straight, with Paulinho just squeezing home.

The road seemed like it was melting most of the day, and there was one point of interest when we passed nearby the field that Lance Armstrong went cyclo-crossing over in 2003. He had to take avoiding action when Joseba Beloki suffered a horrible crash descending, as he skidded on what appeared to be melting tarmac. It was a rare moment when things didn't go quite to plan for Lance in one of his Tour-winning years, but he kept cool, rode across the field, dismounted to negotiate a ditch and then rejoined the race as it came around a hairpin bend.

Mind you, the memory of that is a bit of a lesson: it still pays to stay a little vigilant, even on so-called relaxed days.

Otherwise it was a strange but not unenjoyable day. After the final day in the Alps I realised I was no longer a contender in the 2010 Tour de France so today was the start of the rest of the Tour in many ways. I've been trying to get my head back together and regroup a bit. It is possible I could come good in the Pyrenees and achieve a top ten finish and that's certainly the positive spin we are trying to put on things. It's happened before, with riders who start in poor form and then build to something better, but frankly I don't feel a major surge of form around the corner. The rest of this tour now is about trying to get to Paris and getting something good for the team.

TEMPERS are beginning to get really frayed in this heat, which is getting worse. Can't remember it being this bad before. People are beginning to lose the plot. Mark Renshaw, Cav's Aussie lead-out man, has just been chucked out of the race for head-butting Julian Dean, the main lead-out man for Tyler Farrar, in the final stages of today's sprint finish. I've just seen the replays on the TV and the temptation is to have a bit of a chuckle; it would be comical if it wasn't potentially so serious. Renshaw didn't have a pop just once but three times. Extraordinary stuff really.

As I wrote a bit earlier in connection with Cav, you have to accept that sprinters are a race apart and a bit bonkers, no matter how sane they

might sometimes appear off their bikes. It goes with the territory, doing what they are doing and putting their bodies on the line so regularly. When they commit to the finish they commit totally and anything can happen. The adrenalin is pumping hard and you will be working on instinct. You haven't got time to have a good think and consider your options, you just react at lightning speed all the time to events happening around you. Renshaw is a quality rider. I first encountered him in 2002 at the Commonwealth Games in Manchester, when he was in the Australia Team Pursuit squad along with Brad McGee, Luke Roberts and Graeme Brown, which broke the world record and beat the England team I was riding for into second place. He is also a pretty decent Madison rider finishing 4th in the 2004 World Championships and was 6th in the 2004 Olympics Points race. With that track background

he definitely knows how to handle himself when it all gets a bit physical and had plenty of gas himself.

Renshaw does a great job leading out Mark, never more so than on the Champs Elysées last year, when he cut the pefect line across the final corner exiting the Place de la Concorde, so much so that they left all the other sprinters for dead and took one and two easing up. His very specific task, what he gets paid for, is to take Cav to the front of the sprint some 200–300 metres out by hook or by crook. Mostly that means by picking good lines and reading the race course best and, of course, using his own exceptional speed to stretch the race beyond the reach of others. Occasionally, though, he almost has to fight a way through and that's what happened here. Renshaw obviously thought that Dean, as he moved from right to left, was squeezing him and Cav, and felt he had to do something. You aren't allowed to take your hands of the handlebars and push and shove – that's an automatic disqualification no matter what the circumstances – so in some ways using your head is the only alternative. It's not unknown by any means, the cycling photographers at the finish are always looking for a clash of heads to snap. There was a famous occasion back in 2003 when Baden Cooke and Robbie McEwen – two more Aussies come to think of it – bashed their way down the Champs Elysées together and managed to avoid disqualification. Cooke won the race that day. A couple of years later I seem to remember Robbie was relegated from third to last in one Tour stage, after head-butting Stuart O'Grady, yet another Aussie would you believe. Going back a bit further I definitely remember reports of Tom Steels throwing a water-bottle at Fred Moncassin during a sprint during the 1997 Tour and getting disqualified.

In many ways I am not without sympathy for Renshaw, he takes great pride in getting the job done for Cav, and I hear Sean Kelly has just been on the TV defending him. And Kelly should know – he spent much of his racing life at the sharp end of finishes like that. But fair or unfair, three head-butts is probably one too many to escape the axe. The officials piled in straight after the stage finish and within 20 minutes he had been kicked out. I don't think he was even given a chance to argue his case.

STEVE CUMMINGS

STEVE is my oldest mate in cycling, well the oldest one who is still cycling at the top level anyway. If Michael Barry is my wing man, Steve is my front guard, working hard up the road either pulling the break back or getting in the break himself. Like Mike, he is a man of unbreakable integrity and high personal standards which he doesn't let slip. He is strong-minded and has no qualms whatsoever at expressing his views and disagreeing with anybody, including management. He also enjoys a laugh and we are still like two kids when we get together. Long may it last. We first met when we contested the semi-final of a National Junior Individual Pursuit back in 1997 and before the race he seemed a pretty menacing hard case from the Wirral with a big reputation. I'm happy to say I managed to catch

realises himself if you ask me, with a massive engine. He won an Olympic silver medal alongside me with the Great Britain team pursuit squad in 2004 and went one better with a gold medal at the 2005 World Championships. After that he turned to a full-time road career and found the going pretty tough, serving spells with the Landbouwkrediet team in Belgium and the mighty Discovery squad. It started to come together when he joined Barloworld, who weren't a super strong team but Steve got plenty of opportunity to ride. He will admit himself that he wasn't at his best on the Tour this year. As for many other riders, the Giro had taken too much out of him, but there will be other Tours.

MENDE

WE finished at an aerodrome today, at about 3500 feet, after a tough day riding through the Massif Central and Ardèche. A so-called transition day. I thought transition days were meant to be easier and relaxing? Today was a rolling stage, with five category climbs, finishing with a nasty ascent up the Mende, which gets very steep at 10 per cent+ in places. Montée Laurent Jalabert they call it, after the Frenchman won on the Tour here on Bastille Day in 1995. Contador loves it up this climb – he rode well here in the Paris–Nice back in March – but Andy Schleck has got a mental block about it. Schleck is a great climber and he has 'conquered' much harder climbs, but this is one of those ascents which just doesn't suit his particular style

and cadence. And if you get a mental hang-up about a climb then it become twice as difficult because you are on the back foot before you start. He was talking before the stage about the need to limit his losses and I would think he would be pretty happy, in fact delighted, with the 10 seconds he lost to Contador. Joaquim Rodriguez won the stage ahead of Contador, with Vinokourov third. Myself and Thomas Lofkvist were just 33 seconds back and I was pleased enough as we had experienced a really tough start, with G crashing and me getting caught up in the chaos. We had to chase back at full bore for over an hour and then it was an up and down day before we arrived at the final climb. All things considered, it wasn't too shabby. On this sort of terrain, when we don't go up beyond that 1500 m ceiling, I am feeling good and pretty competitive.

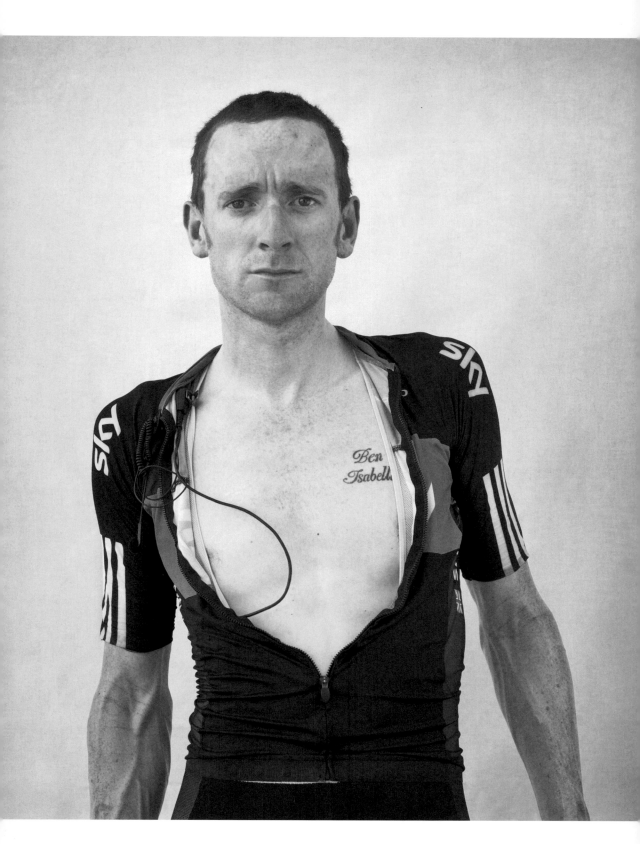

RORY GALLAGHER, TATTOOED LADY; 'A' BOMB IN WARDOUR STREET, THE JAM; THE WORLD IS YOURS, IAN
FEELGOOD; RUN THROUGH THE JUNGLE, CREEDENCE CLEARWATER REVIVAL; ALL I WANNA DO (IS BE WITH
THE SMITHS; STELLIFY, IAN BROWN; THE ETON RIFLES, THE JAM; MY EVER CHANGING MOODS [SINGLE EI
JOY DIVISION; ALL THE KING'S MEN, WILD BEASTS; LEAVING HERE, THE WHO, THIS CHARMING MAN, THE
JAM; YOU NEVER CAN TELL (SOUNDTRACK VERSION WITH DIALOGUE), CHUCK BERRY; DON'T GO CHANG
UNDERGROUND, THE JAM; SOME MIGHT SAY, OASIS; THREE BUTTON HAND ME DOWN, FACES; SUNFLOWE
KAISER CHIEFS; SOUND OF THE SUBURBS, THE MEMBERS; I'M GOING HOME, TEN YEARS AFTER, LIVE AT THE
KASABIAN; FROM THE FLOORBOARDS UP, PAUL WELLER; PARACHUTE WOMAN [LIVE], THE ROLLING STONE
FIRE, KASABIAN; ROCK 'N' ROLL STAR, OASIS; JUST A LITTLE MISUNDERSTANDING, THE CONTOURS; WHAT
TURN UP THE SUN, OASIS; LA BELLE ET LA BÊTE, BABYSHAMBLES; BILLERICAY DICKIE, IAN DURY; TO BE S
HEROES, DAVID BOWIE; SPARKS, THE WHO; YOU'RE THE BEST THING [SINGLE EDIT], PAUL WELLER & THE
ADORED, THE STONE ROSES; DON'T LOOK BACK IN ANGER, OASIS; I'M THE FACE, THE HIGH NUMBERS; S
IN THE TUBE STATION AT MIDNIGHT, THE JAM; L.S.F., KASABIAN; PRETTY VACANT, THE SEX PISTOLS; TIME
STONES); SLIDE AWAY, OASIS; BOY WITH THE BLUES; LIVE FOREVER OASIS; LOVE SPREADS, THE STONE R
BLOC PARTY; F.E.A.R., IAN BROWN; FLYING, FACES; I BELIEVE IN ALL, OASIS; HAPPY DAYS TOY TOWN [MONO
THE SMITHS; GLASGOW LOVE THEME, CRAIG ARMSTRONG; SOUL KITCHEN, THE DOORS; PRIVATE HELL, TH
JAM; LYLA; OASIS; SPEAK LIKE A CHILD, PAUL WELLER & THE STYLE COUNCIL; DAVID WATTS, THE JAM;
MAN, THE ROLLING STONES; ROADHOUSE BLUES, THE DOORS; THERE'S A GHOST IN MY HOUSE, R. DEAN
BAD 'N' RUIN, FACES; SEX ON FIRE, KINGS OF LEON; THE CHANGINGMAN, PAUL WELLER; WHOLE LOTTA LO
SELLS SANCTUARY, THE CULT; TOWN CALLED MALICE, THE JAM; GET UP (I FEEL LIKE BEING A) SEX MACHIN
NAME, PAUL WELLER; RAMBLE ON, LED ZEPPELIN; BRON-Y-AUR STOMP, LED ZEPPELIN; HARRY KIDNAP, O

RORY GALLAGHER, TATTOOED LADY; 'A' BOMB IN WARDOUR
OYEH!, DR FEELGOOD; SHE DOES IT RIGHT, DR FEELGOOD; F
LONG TALL SALLY, LITTLE RICHARD; WHAT DIFFERENCE D
CHANGING MOODS [SINGLE EDIT], PAUL WELLER & THE STY
MEN, WILD BEASTS; LEAVING HERE, THE WHO, THIS CHARM
THE CITY; THE JAM; YOU NEVER CAN TELL (SOUNDTRACK VE
LAZY SUNDAY (MONO VERSION), SMALL FACES; GOING

PLAYLIST
LISTENED TO ON A LOOP
THROUGHOUT THE 2010 TOUR

I HEARD IT THROUGH THE GRAPEVINE, CREEDENCE CLEARWATER REVIVAL; NEVER MISS A BEAT
1970; ALL ABLAZE, IAN BROWN; I WANNA BE YOUR DOG (REMASTERED), THE STOOGES; UNDERGRO
& ROCK & ROLL, IAN DURY; COME ON/LET'S GO!, PAUL WELLER; LUCY THE CASTLE THE TWO WHEELERS
TO MY ROCK 'N' ROLL (PUNK SONG), BLACK REBEL MOTORCYCLE CLUB; DISORDER, JOY DIVISION, TURN U
LAZY SUNDAY (09/04/1968 JOHN PEEL SESSION), SMALL FACES; INTO TOMORROW, PAUL WELLER; DIT
TIN SOLDIER, THE SMALL FACES; THE BOY WITH THE THORN IN HIS SIDE, THE SMITHS; I WANNA BE ADOR
DIVISION; A BELL WILL RING, OASIS; EVERYDAY I LOVE YOU LESS AND LESS, KAISER CHIEFS; DOWN IN T
IAN BROWN; JUMPIN' JACK FLASH (LIVE WITH JOHN LENNON'S INTRODUCTION OF THE ROLLING STONES)
THE SMITHS; L.A. WOMAN, THE DOORS; THE MODERN WORLD, THE JAM; TWO MORE YEARS, BLOC PARTY;
ARE YOU GONNA BE MY GIRL? JET; ROCK, COFFEE & TV, BLUR; BIGMOUTH STRIKES AGAIN, THE SMITHS;
THE JAM; HEATWAVE (STEREO), MARTHA REEVES & THE VANDELLAS; THICK AS THIEVES, THE JAM; LYLA
MONKEYS; THE HEADMASTER RITUAL, THE SMITHS; LET THERE BE LOVE, OASIS; MONKEY MAN, THE ROL
THE UNDERTONES; SUZIE Q, CREEDENCE CLEARWATER REVIVAL; FALLING DOWN, OASIS; BAD 'N' RUIN, FA
MORNING RAIN, PAUL WELLER; TRANSMISSION, JOY DIVISION; STAY WITH ME, FACES; SHE SELLS SANCTU
LA LA, THE FACES; COLUMBIA (LIVE FROM THE CHICAGO METRO) OASIS; 7&3 IS THE STRIKERS NAME, PAU
ON KEEPING ON, NOLAN PORTER; TOMMY'S HOLIDAY CAMP, THE WHO; UNCLE ERNIE, THE WHO. LUST F

CAN'T YOU HEAR ME KNOCKING?, THE ROLLING STONES; OYEH!, DR FEELGOOD; SHE DOES IT RIGHT, DR
L WELLER; LONG TALL SALLY, LITTLE RICHARD; WHAT DIFFERENCE DOES IT MAKE? (PEEL SESSION, BBC),
WELLER & THE STYLE COUNCIL; GHOSTS, THE JAM; 2-4-6-8 MOTORWAY, TOM ROBINSON BAND; DIGITAL,
S! SOMEBODY, KINGS OF LEON; LOVE IS NOISE, THE VERVE; LUST FOR LIFE, IGGY POP; IN THE CITY; THE
OONS; THE IMPORTANCE OF BEING IDLE, OASIS; LAZY SUNDAY (MONO VERSION), SMALL FACES; GOING
ELLER; I HEARD IT THROUGH THE GRAPEVINE, CREEDENCE CLEARWATER REVIVAL; NEVER MISS A BEAT,
E EAST, 1970; ALL ABLAZE, IAN BROWN; I WANNA BE YOUR DOG (REMASTERED), THE STOOGES; UNDERDOG,
RUGS & ROCK & ROLL, IAN DURY; COME ON/LET'S GO!, PAUL WELLER; LUCY THE CASTLE, TWISTED WHEEL;
PENED TO MY ROCK 'N' ROLL (PUNK SONG), BLACK REBEL MOTORCYCLE CLUB; DISORDER, JOY DIVISION;
E JAM; LAZY SUNDAY (03/04/1968 JOHN PEEL SESSION), SMALL FACES; INTO TOMORROW, PAUL WELLER;
NCIL; TIN SOLDIER, THE SMALL FACES; THE BOY WITH THE THORN IN HIS SIDE, THE SMITHS; I WANNA BE
, JOY DIVISION; A BELL WILL RING, OASIS; EVERYDAY I LOVE YOU LESS AND LESS, KAISER CHIEFS; DOWN
YTHING, IAN BROWN; JUMPIN' JACK FLASH (LIVE WITH JOHN LENNON'S INTRODUCTION OF THE ROLLING
D IN GLOVE, THE SMITHS; L.A. WOMAN, THE DOORS; THE MODERN WORLD, THE JAM; TWO MORE YEARS,
SMALL FACES; ARE YOU GONNA BE MY GIRL? JET; ROCK, COFFEE & TV, BLUR; BIGMOUTH STRIKES AGAIN,
TTY GREEN, THE JAM; HEATWAVE (STEREO), MARTHA REEVES & THE VANDELLAS; THICK AS THIEVES, THE
VOUR, ARCTIC MONKEYS; THE HEADMASTER RITUAL, THE SMITHS; LET THERE BE LOVE, OASIS; MONKEY
EENAGE KICKS, THE UNDERTONES; SUZIE Q, CREEDENCE CLEARWATER REVIVAL; FALLING DOWN, OASIS;
PEEL); EARLY MORNING RAIN, PAUL WELLER; TRANSMISSION, JOY DIVISION; STAY WITH ME; FACES; SHE
BROWN; OOH LA LA, THE FACES; COLUMBIA (LIVE FROM THE CHICAGO METRO) OASIS; 7&3 IS THE STRIKERS
UR; KEEP ON KEEPING ON, NOLAN PORTER; TOMMY'S HOLIDAY CAMP, THE WHO; UNCLE ERNIE, THE WHO.
THE JAM; THE WORLD IS YOURS, IAN BROWN; CAN'T YOU HEAR ME KNOCKING?, THE ROLLING STONES;
GH THE JUNGLE, CREEDENCE CLEARWATER REVIVAL; ALL I WANNA DO (IS BE WITH YOU), PAUL WELLER;
KE? (PEEL SESSION, BBC), THE SMITHS; STELLIFY, IAN BROWN; THE ETON RIFLES, THE JAM; MY EVER
L; GHOSTS, THE JAM; 2-4-6-8 MOTORWAY, TOM ROBINSON BAND; DIGITAL, JOY DIVISION; ALL THE KING'S
THE MOONS; USE SOMEBODY, KINGS OF LEON; LOVE IS NOISE, THE VERVE; LUST FOR LIFE, IGGY POP; IN
H D? ROUBELL, CHUCK BERRY; DON'T GO/HANGIN', THE MOONS; THE IMPORTANCE OF BEING IDLE, OASIS;
THE JAM; SOME MIGHT SAY, OASIS; THREE BUTTON HAND ME DOWN, FACES; SUNFLOWER, PAUL WELLER;
UND OF THE SUBURBS, THE MEMBERS; I'M GOING HOME, TEN YEARS AFTER, LIVE AT THE FILLMORE EAST,
THE FLOORBOARDS UP, PAUL WELLER; PARACHUTE WOMAN (LIVE), THE ROLLING STONES; SEX & DRUGS
ROCK 'N' ROLL STAR, OASIS; JUST A LITTLE MISUNDERSTOOD, THE CONTOURS; WHATEVER HAPPENED
ASIS; A BELLE ET LA BÊTE, BABYSHAMBLES; BILLERICAY DICKIE, IAN DURY; TO BE SOMEONE, THE JAM;
E SHARKS, THE WHO; YOU'RE THE BEST THING (SINGLE EDIT), PAUL WELLER & THE STYLE COUNCIL;
O E ROSES; DON'T LOOK BACK IN ANGER, OASIS; I'M THE FACE, THE HIGH NUMBERS; SHADOWPLAY, JOY
ON AT MIDNIGHT, THE JAM; L.S.F., KASABIAN; PRETTY VACANT, SEX PISTOLS; TIME IS MY EVERYTHING,
OASIS; MAN WITH THE BLUES; LIVE FOREVER, OASIS; LOVE SPREADS, THE STONE ROSES; HAND IN GLOVE,
BROWN; FLYING, FACES; I BELIEVE IN ALL, OASIS; ITCHYCOO TOWN (MONO VERSION), SMALL FACES;
HE THEME, CRAIG ARMSTRONG; SOUL KITCHEN, THE DOORS; PRIVATE HELL, THE JAM; PRETTY GREEN,
E ONCE A CHILD, PAUL WELLER & THE STYLE COUNCIL; GHOSTS, THE JAM; DO ME A FAVOUR, ARCTIC
ES; ROADHOUSE BLUES, THE DOORS; THERE'S A GHOST IN MY HOUSE, R. DEAN TAYLOR; TEENAGE KICKS,
N FIRE, KINGS OF LEON; THE CHANGINGMAN, PAUL WELLER; WHOLE LOTTA LOVE, LED ZEPPELIN; EARLY
ULT; TOWN CALLED MALICE, THE JAM; GET UP (I FEEL LIKE BEING A) SEX MACHINE, JAMES BROWN; OOH
RAMBLE ON, LED ZEPPELIN; BRON-Y-AUR STOMP, LED ZEPPELIN; HARRY KIDNAP, OCEAN COLOUR; KEEP
GY POP; IN THE CITY; THE JAM; YOU NEVER CAN TELL (SOUNDTRACK VERSION WITH DIALOGUE), CHUCK

REVEL

Novotel Toulouse Aéroport, Blagnac
Also in residence: Lampre

TWO nights in the same hotel, a rare luxury
and a rare glimpse of a major city – we are on
the outskirts of Toulouse – in what has been a
particularly rural Tour this year, apart from the
opening days in Holland and Belgium. We are by the
airport at, shall we say, a functional hotel. There
have been lots of emotional ups and downs again;
this Tour is perplexing me. On Saturday, from Rodez
to Revel, I felt great and am kicking myself for not
taking advantage. It was an undulating course,
three category fours and two category threes,
including quite a steep little Côte de Saint Ferreol,
5 miles from home. Up the final climb Alessandro
Ballan went off, followed by Vino, and I should
have reacted. I felt absolutely fine and could have

comfortably gone with them, and then who knows
what might have happened? I felt so strong all day
and at the finish. Great legs. On the descent and
the run home Vino powered away and won, while
the bunch sprint was taken by Cav, who fought
hard for those points, with EBH taking fourth for
us, another good effort from him. That's three top
five finishes for him now. Shame about that early
season injury, which has left him just a bit short,
but he is young and his time will come. I'm kicking
myself though. Why didn't I go with Vino? I suppose
I'm lacking confidence generally. I started the Tour
as a GC contender and as a GC contender there was
no need to get involved in a dust-up at the front.
A proper GC contender would do exactly what the
likes of Contador and Schleck did and sit in the
bunch, keep out of trouble as we make our way to
the Pyrenees and roll home with us 31 seconds,

I think it was, later. But I am not a GC contender any more and shouldn't be thinking like one any more in this race. I should have been much more opportunistic and on the look out for the chance of a stage win. I can justify not going for it by arguing that we were working for a stage win for EBH, but once that break went it was unlikely it was going to end in a bunch finish for victory. We had missed that. I'm annoyed. A rider like me doesn't get that many opportunities to sniff a stage win on a Grand Tour, away from prologues and time-trials; Grand Tours are set up for sprinters and climbers, and I should have had a dart. And then, today, from Revel to Ax-3 Domaines.

Back into the mountains again and the start of four days in the Pyrenees. Two big climbs today – the Port de Pailhères, which is nearly 16 km at 8 per cent and tops out at 2001 m, and then a sharp

climb into Aix-3 Domaines, although it was much lower there finishing at just under 1400 m. What can I say? From feeling terrific but frustrated on the Saturday riding into Revel, I suddenly felt poor again as we hit the heights on the first main climb. I just had nothing extra to give. I was trying but nothing happened. There was no point in Thomas waiting for me this time, he rode ahead to finish 2 minutes 30 secs behind the winner, Christophe Riblon, with me 4 mins 59 secs adrift of the winner. It's a bloody tough climb, the Pailhères. It's pretty new to the Tour – it made its debut in 2003 I think – but it's a pretty typical Pyrenean brute. The gradients are really uneven, there's no one stretch which stays constant so a bigger climber can use their power and just grind it out. You have to keep swtiching cadence and gears, standing up on the pedals, sitting down on the saddle. It's all very

testing and the hairpins don't really come where
you would expect them either, so it's a struggle
to get into a rhythm. To be honest, it was just a
struggle – end of story – today. It's exactly the sort
of climb I don't like. Nice descent into Ax-les-
Thermes though. Down at the finish I stopped for a
moment before riding back down the mountain and
one of the guys I saw in the press pack was John
'Iffy' Trevorrow, an old friend of my late father Garry
from Australia. I hadn't really intended to stop for
a press call – everybody could see for themselves
what had happened and I was no longer a factor
on the Tour – but Iffy stepped forward and asked
me the obvious really – why wasn't I able to go with
the leaders' pace, why was I going along at my own
speed? Suddenly it all came out. I felt tired and
pretty emotional: 'Want me to be honest with you
Iffy?' I said. 'I'm fucked mate. I've got nothing left.

I just don't have the form, it's as simple as that.
I'm not going to lie to you, I am trying my hardest,
battling on rather than giving up. I just haven't got it
like I had it last year and I don't know why. I just feel
consistently mediocre. Not brilliant, not shit, just
mediocre.'

I knew this wasn't my year when we left the
Alps but today was confirmation that I am not
improving in any way and won't be able to rally in
the Pyrenees and recover a bit of lost ground. I'm
not sure it isn't the most depressing day of all. This
year I am simply not able to go with those at the
front and pride stops me dropping right down the
field and tapping along in the grupetto. A lonely no-
man's land really, and plenty of time to mull it all
over and curse away to myself trying to work it all
out. I'm not going to deny that thoughts of chucking
it all in don't come into your mind on such days.

You are close to breaking point much of the time on the Tour, but the thought is normally only fleeting. There is your pride and reputation to uphold, there is all the hard work of the team and support of your loved ones to remember, and, for those of us who have got around before, the memories of that fantastic moment when you arrive in Paris is also a strong incentive. We are professional cyclists and the urge is always to get the job done.

So you grit your teeth and get on with it. Just concentrate on the road ahead and don't let your mind start dwelling on all the climbs to come. Another 100 metres. And another 100 metres. Look up for a moment, take the crowd in, try to feed off their energy. Head down again. Another 100 metres, and another 100 metres. Head up again. This time count 50 pedal strokes: 50 left, 50 right. And again. Head up, breathe deeply. Try to keep that breathing

under control. Don't hyperventilate, stay in a calm smooth place if possible. You can't ride without oxygen. Head down. Another 100 metres. Another 50 pedal strokes left, another 50 right. Just keep going. Get to the finish and the bus. The bus is your goal today, not the winning line. There is no glory today. Just the bus. You can rest there Brad, it will be all right in the bus. Your day can end there. As you go around a corner you might see three or four British fans, who have probably been waiting since early morning, waving the flag and cheering you on. You can't let them down. Another 100 metres. And another. You are in a world of your own.

Eventually you collapse over the line, or lean on somebody's shoulder for support. You have made it, somehow. Another sweltering day in the mountains. You head for the bus – ice packs, a shower, a rice recovery meal, collapse in your chair. Gradually

the news of the day starts filtering through and you might see some newsclips on the TV in the bus.

Contador and Schleck seemed to be having some fun today, sprinting up the climb and then stalling like you do on the track, probing for a weakness in the other. That ability to 'mess around' on such steep gradients is pretty special but ultimately it ended in stalemate, both riders coming in just over a minute behind Christophe Riblon and taking no time out of each other. In their own minds it is clearly a two-horse race and they are probably right; if they had been worried about anybody else they would have forged ahead and built an even bigger lead at the top of the GC.

The air-con is belting out but I still feel like I am burning up. This heat is slowly sending everybody around the bend. I forgot to mention Rui Costa and Carlos Barredo went at it hammer and tongs for no good reason I have heard about at the end of stage 6. They got fined but were photographed shaking hands and making up at the start line the next day. It's just the Tour; it can do your head in sometimes and, when it all gets too much, the temptation is often just to lash out at the nearest person.

PORT DE BALÈS

Novotel Toulouse Aéroport, Blagnac
Also in residence: Lampre

TODAY was a big day – both literally out there on the road and in the eventual outcome of the 2010 Tour de France. The route – Pamiers to Bagnères-de-Luchon – is a classic Pyrenean ride, taking in the Col de Portet-d'Aspet, the Col des Ares and then the big one, the HC Port de Balès, which is a 19 km pig of a climb with some really nasty stretches.

The Col de Portet-d'Aspet has been in the Tour since 1910, when the race first visited the Pyrenees, and its appearance this year is part of the Centenary celebrations. It's another trademark Pyrenean climb, particularly at the top where it steepens to 10 per cent, but it sometimes seems a sinister climb as well. Much of the climb and descent is through the treeline, which is both good and bad. There is plenty of shade on hot sunny days, which is good but can become a bit of a nightmare when it's wet and the road becomes particularly slippery. It was on the descent during a stage in 1995 that the Barcelona Olympic champion Fabio Casartelli lost his life. He was going flat out after the steepest section of the descent – a 17 per cent stretch – when he lost control at a bend, slid across the road and smashed his head against one of those big square blocks of concrete that are placed alongside the tops of ravines to stop cars plunging over the side. He died on the way to hospital. It's not something you want to dwell on too much when you descend, but, when you think about it, there are remarkably few accidents considering the risks we take and the speed at which we travel. Riding at speed in the peloton is a real skill and is probably the thing the talented amateur cyclist out

there would find most difficult. You can have all the fitness and speed and endurance in the world, but if you can't ride surrounded by another 150 riders you are going to struggle. The merest touch of the brakes or swerve at the wrong time and you will cause carnage. The sheer bike handling skills of most of my professional colleagues is extraordinary really. You can get transfixed by those pictures from the helicopter, when you watch an echelon moving across the road in windy conditions or when you see the peloton pouring into a tight narrow bend. It thinks and moves as one, like a flock of starlings wheeling around at sunset. That can only happen if you have 190 world-class cyclists all focused on what they are doing. Just one mistake or miscalculation from one rider and most of us will come tumbling down. Of course we do sometimes come tumbling down, but the wonder is that it

doesn't happen much more often.

There is now a stone and marble memorial to Casartelli at the site of his crash, a sundial by the looks of it, and I am told a hole has been drilled through the base of the stone so that each year, at exactly the time Casartelli died, the sun shines through the hole and illuminates some figures that are engraved on the other face of the stone. Apparently those figures are his date of birth, the date he won Olympic gold and the date he died.

In terms of the race we all know that Andy Schleck has to go on the attack and today, potentially, was quite promising. Tomorrow is definitely not so good because there is a massive 60 km run-off after the last climb, which a well organised team will chase down, so that just leaves the Tourmalet summit finish on Thursday. So the scene was set and by all accounts the yellow jersey

fight up the front was pretty 'interesting', although I suffered one of my worst days yet and finished well off the pace, 9 mins 35 secs behind Thomas Voeckler, who won with a fine breakaway effort. The French are having a good Tour.

The drama, though, was all around the yellow jersey group, with Contador marking Andy Schleck very closely. I haven't seen the footage yet and it's probably pointless me commenting until I have, but it seems Andy went on the attack and put about 50 yards into Contador, who countered. Schleck then

had some sort of mechanical but Contador kept going and eventually put 39 seconds into Schleck, who had to stop to fix the problem, taking the yellow jersey off him.

Just read that Bagnères-de-Luchon is twin-towned with Harrogate. Can't remember any 2000m mountains in that part of Yorkshire, but I might be mistaken.

CHAIN REACTION

RIGHT I've seen the footage and I'm tempted to say 'told you so' following my comments after the Spa stage about so-called conventions and traditions in the Tour de France. I won't go down that road but let's just say I can't believe all this fuss and media attention to the 39 seconds Alberto Contador gained on Andy Schleck today after apparently 'attacking' Andy in the yellow jersey when he suffered a mechanical problem with his chain. Who says it's a convention that the yellow jersey can't be attacked when he messes up on a gear change or encounters an everyday problem? It's not as if he was knocked flat by a mad fan running alongside, or got put in a ditch by some rank bad bike handling from somebody else in the Astana team! If you just study the footage for a couple of minutes there is no case to answer. The Tour de France is now clearly a two-horse race – Andy v Alberto – and Andy in

yellow made his big attack of the day. He did look strong, and the way he chased back after the mechanical suggests to me that he felt today was the day he could finally put time into Alberto, which is probably why he was so angry afterwards which was not typical of the man. Andy is a very cool and fair-minded guy – a really good bloke – but I don't think he has much to complain about. Alberto responded to his attack and was sprinting up the climb chasing back when something happened with Andy's chain. It could well have been a badly timed gear change on his part or it could have been a mechanical problem that was either bad luck or perhaps down to the team and their suppliers, but my point is exactly the same as the one I made thousands of miles away in Spa. It's just the fortunes of war and we shouldn't be trying to overly protect the big names by unwritten conventions and

traditions which seem to be used by all and sundry for their own purposes. When Alberto went around Andy as he was beginning to slow down was he really meant to brake to a halt and politely ask what was happening? I seem to remember Andy riding tactically in the mountains the other day, slowing right down and almost stopping like the sprinters do on the track before heading off again. He could have been doing that for all Contador knew. As far as he was concerned, the gauntlet had been thrown down and he was picking it up. The press and TV are going mad but it was all fair and above board. It was man on man with the Tour de France title up for grabs. It's not a bloody tea-party. That was the race right there. Andy made a move, Alberto responded strongly, Andy either made a cock-up or got a bit unlucky for a minute. It happens. In a Wimbledon final you see players apologising profusely to their opponent when they get an unlucky net cord or bad bounce, but not once in the history of tennis do I remember them ever offering to play the point again. Just get on with it guys, it's road racing. There was no need for Alberto to do anything other than thank his slice of luck and keep going. I don't think I am alone in this view. My old colleague at Garmin-Transitions, Ryder Hesjedal, seems to have summed it up well: 'If you draw your sword and drop it, you will die.' Carlos Sastre was giving out the other day and I know where he is coming from: 'I've had technical problems and nobody ever waited for me. We are turning cycling into a sport of spoiled brats.' Stuff happens, deal with it.

PAU

Hotel Campanile – Pau
Also in residence: Footon-Servetto

RELAXING down here on the outskirts of Pau as the rain beats down. It feels like the weather has broken at last, two and a half weeks into the Tour. A strange old day to report. An epic day in many respects, with four classic Pyrenean climbs and hours of endless climbing, yet in the final analysis it has absolutely no bearing on the race itself. For all the effect it had on the 2010 Tour de France we might as well have not bothered.

It started bizarrely with an apology from Alberto, filmed overnight by somebody at Astana and posted on YouTube. Unnecessary and over the top. No apology was required. *L'Equipe* had a picture of Contador in yellow on the podium last night winking 'Contador san pitié' – 'Ruthless Contador' is the

translation. I'm happy with that. Winning sportsmen are often ruthless. In retrospect, his only mistake, in the heat of the moment, when immediately grilled by the press, was to deny he has seen Schleck in trouble. From the tape it is quite clear he had to take avoiding action to miss going into the man in yellow. He should have owned up to that, but there was still no need for him to stop.

Today we fought our way up the Peyresourde, the Col d'Aspin, the Tourmalet and finally the Col du Souloir and the Col d'Aubisque – that's got to be 70 km of climbing – but in the end the massive 59 km descent into Pau saw no major gains or losses result. In many ways it felt like a Queen stage when you looked at the profile in the road book and took in all the historic names, but it needed to end on top of the Aubisque for that really to be the case. I was in a good frame of mind this morning, after two

Col de Tourmalet

Passage au point de la Giaillae bridge
km 166.9

1 140m Barèges - km 161.9

D 918 - D 140 - km 158.4

or three tough days when I don't mind admitting it was sometimes difficult to keep focus. I'm completely out of contention as far as the top of the GC is concerned so there was a chance I could get in the break and Lance was pretty much the same as well. Plus I fancied Lance was going to make one final big effort in the mountains before his Tour career comes to an end and today was always the strongest contender. It is the most 'romantic' stage of the Tour, with all the big climbs and possibly the biggest crowd, plus the final day on the Tourmalet will be all about Alberto Contador and Andy Schleck. That will be a very controlled day, setting up the big shoot-out at the death. No, if Lance was going to make a break, I had worked out it would be today. And so it nearly came to pass. We virtually sprinted up the Peyresourde, 11 km straight up into the heavens, which was certainly a tough start to a

long day. We really got stuck in, giving it everything, and a break of 14–15 riders slowly got away; but to be honest the break was too strong a group for the peloton to allow us too much leeway. We were out the front but it didn't really mean a huge amount. They caught us on the Tourmalet but then Lance went off again in a smaller break and this time it was for real. Carlos Barredo attacked early in the ascent of the Aubisque and it all got pretty lively, other members of the break not running him down until the flamme rouge, which is always 1 km from the finish. After that it was an all-French affair, Pierrick Fedrigo just sneaking it from Sandy Casar. There was no fairytale ending for Lance, who has never really had a sprint finish, and he trailed off into sixth, but it has been a brave last throw of the dice and probably his last truly competitive ride in the Tour de France. A good way to sign off. It also

confirmed what I have thought throughout this last
three weeks: he might be nearly 39 but he is very fit
this year and could have done well in the GC given
some luck. I came home with the bunch at 6 mins
45 secs behind and was pleased enough with that.

PYRENEAN QUEENS

THE ORGANISERS, who have made a big thing of 2010 being the centenary of the Tour de France, including Pyrenean climbs on the route, threw the kitchen sink at us on stage 16, with four of the classic climbs from the region which appeared in a famous stage back in 1910. Scenically it was probably the best stage of the Tour, although when you are head down sweating away the moment is lost on you a little. Tactically it lost its impact because there was 60 km of descent at the end to recoup your losses, but for Tour aficionados it was still a day to savour.

The Peyresourde might look beautiful and rustic first up in the fresh morning air – indeed, some riders describe it as their favourite climb – but they must be thinking of a quiet training day. When you are racing in the Tour de France it takes no prisoners whatsoever. It veers from

anything between 4 and 10 per cent, it never settles into a steady rise, and after the village of Garin it becomes twisty and difficult. I remember Vino doing one of his Lazarus acts here in 2007. He had taken a bad fall early in the Tour and had stitches, hampering the movement of his knee, but he led the peloton over the Peyresourde and held on in the descent down to Loudenvielle. A couple of days later came his infamous time-trial at Albi, and a couple of days later he was kicked off the Tour.

Next up on this nostalgic stage was the Col d'Aspin, one of the orginal climbs in 1910 and a pleasant not too demanding ascent these days – 12 km at less than 4 per cent, although there is a nasty little steep section just after mid way. You try and just switch off here and tap out a good rhythm – and gather yourself for what you know lies ahead – the Tourmalet.

The Tourmalet, I suppose, is the iconic Pyrenean climb. It's the highest at 2115 m and is normally only open from late May to early October. It is also probably the most consistently difficult, with no real let up over the 17 km. There is also a sort of natural amphitheatre as you reach the top and the biggest crowds always gather there, either taking up station days ahead in their camper vans or rising at dawn and walking up on the day. It's an amazing sight. And it is a proper mountain top finish – a few metres after you reach the line and pass the summit restaurant you plunge back down into the valley.

It was on the lower slopes of the Tourmalet that a famous incident took place in 1913 when Eugène Christophe had to walk down 10 km with his bike on his shoulders after his handlebars broke to find a blacksmith in St-Marie de Campan. There, under the rules of the day, he had to make his own repairs and was docked a further 10 minutes by officials when a young girl helped him by using a blacksmith's bellows.

To finish off a pretty epic segment of the Pyrenees we end with the twin peaks of Col du Souloir and the Col d'Aubisque. It was on the Aubisque that the first rider over in 1910, Octave Lapize, angrily accused one of the organisers – sports journalist Alphonse Steines – of being an 'assassin' for organising such a murderous climb on the Tour. It always seems pretty wild at the top of the Aubisque, you can get plenty of dodgy weather and it is famous for its wild horses and cattle. On the Souloir you are more likely to get donkeys.

The first part of the descent isn't too clever. Back in 1951 the race leader Wim van Est went over the side and had his fall halted by a tree. His Dutch team then knotted all their spare inner tubes

together to make a rope to successfully haul him up. Unfortunately that meant none of the tubes then fitted the rims of their wheels and they soon had to abandon the race. I have another good reason to remember the Aubisque, but we might come to that later.

The terrain on stage 16 is pretty much the route ridden by Eddy Merckx during possibly his greatest moment, on his debut Tour in 1969 when he absolutely crucified the peloton on stage 17 from Luchon to Mourenx. Something had annoyed Merckx and he had vowed to friends that he would pick the hardest stage of the Tour – stage 17 – to make his point. There was no need to, he had been comfortably in yellow since stage 6 but he took off at the top of the Tourmalet on that brilliant fast descent to Barèges and that was the last anybody saw of him. He continued to attack on his own all

the way up the Aubisque and was nearly 8 minutes ahead at the finish. And all this from the man already in the yellow jersey. Incredible. It was after that ride that a *L'Equipe* journo coined the term 'Merckxissimo' and the press generally dubbed him the Cannibal because of his voracious appetite for victory. He was nearly 18 minutes ahead by the time the race reached Paris. He won the yellow jersey, the mountains competition, the points jersey and of course what they used to call the combined jersey as well. It barely seems credible that one rider could do all that.

REST DAY #2

Hotel Campanile – Pau
Also in residence: Footon-Servetto

IT'S late afternoon and absolutely dripping with rain here at the Campanile. It's gone cold as well, almost autumnal, but that's fine by me. No dramas or excitement today and I can feel my body relaxing a bit. I've been wandering around the hotel compound barefoot and stripped to my waist just enjoying the coolness and freshness of the day.

There is nothing much left in this race for us now, although I am going to give it a good whack at the time-trial on Saturday. There's a pretty melancholy end-of-the-race feeling around generally, although the actual yellow jersey will be on the line when Andy Schleck and Alberto Contador go head to head on the Tourmalet tomorrow. Ascension Thursday, as *L'Equipe* is

already calling it. Andy will win the stage but there is no way he will ever put enough time into Alberto to have any chance at Saturday's time-trial. You read it here first!

Went out for a very gentle spin with the lads about 11 a.m. this morning, before the rain really set in. Sean Yates joined us and although we were spinning gently along he insisted on grinding it out in one of his big gears! At one point we were also joined by a weekend warrior on a mountain bike, in shorts and wearing trainers, who got his head down and blasted on ahead of us and will no doubt be dining out on yarns of burning off Sky for a month or two. Good luck to him. At one point Rod Ellingworth in our team car even pulled alongside him to offer the guy an energy bar or a drink.

Pulled over mid-ride and switched to my time-trial bike to get the feel again before Saturday's TT

Worked hard for a short period to test myself and build up a sweat. Good, happy with the set up and position, and felt strong when I really upped the pace. Perhaps we can finish on a high after all. Will resist the temptation to put in a final 'do or die' ride up the Tourmalet tomorrow in an attempt to scrape into the top 20 GC, which would be for appearances sake only and fool nobody. I'm really not bothered if I finish 19th or 29th at this stage, but I do want to put in a decent TT for my own pride after the prologue in Rotterdam. We've had a good look at the course and it could be a good one for me. It's the right distance, 52 km, and no hills as such. The wind off the Gironne estuary could well be a factor, apparently it gets up in the afternoon, but that's beyond my control so I am not thinking about it.

Had a chat with a French family when we got back into the Campanile compound and showed them around and signed a few bit and pieces – Shane Sutton had noticed their interest when they were looking around and I was more than happy to oblige. They seemed interested and grateful.

The travelling British fans have been great as well, the best thing of this Tour for me. The temptation has been to keep my head down and avoid them this last week or so, since I have been out of contention. I've felt really embarrassed and bad about letting them down but everywhere I go they have been fantastically supportive. 'Keep going Brad, you're a hero', 'Keep fighting Brad, we are with you all the way', all that kind of stuff which really humbles you. No recriminations or slaggings off. Wish I could have given them a bit more to shout about but maybe next year. They are over here, hopefully having a good time, supporting a British team and their man, and are staying loyal to the cause. It's been a big surprise to us how we have attracted this fan base so quickly, and it's up to us to give them something to really cheer about in the years ahead. There are a lot of British Tour de France fans out there and having a team to shout for, good or bad, seems to be helping their enjoyment of the entire race.

Thomas Lofkvist went and did another hour on the turbo trainer when we got in but it was a shower and kip for me, a bit of music and any moment now I will go over to the restaurant area and do some press – much happier about that prospect than earlier in the Tour. I will tell them exactly what I think and give them an honest assessment of my Tour in particular and Sky's Tour in general. Dinner about 8 p.m., a bit of a mooch around and then an early night. Last big day in the mountains tomorrow.

Happily, it's been an uneventful stay so far in Pau, very low key, which makes a nice change to be honest. The last time I was here I was 'arrested' by the Gendarmerie at the top of the Aubisque, given a police escort back to Pau nick – flashing lights, police outriders, the full works – had my room searched by their specialist drugs squad and 'escaped' to the airport early the following morning wearing Dave Millar's Saunier Dauval top by way of disguise. It was a miserable time, probably the all-time low of my career. For a while I didn't just not want to ride the Tour, I wanted nothing to do with road cycling. I headed for home seriously wondering if I wanted anything more to do with the sport.

My Cofidis colleague Cristian Moreni – a guy I had actually got on with pretty well – tested positive for testosterone so of course the rest of the team got caught up in the nonsense and were kicked off the Tour. I was innocent of all charges, I will never abuse my body and cheat by taking drugs, but there is always that fear that the public will look on you differently – that guilt by association thing – and I hated every mad moment of that time in Pau. Police everywhere, photographers taking pictures of me being led away at the finish and then chasing you for pictures at the police station and the team hotel. And of course all the time you can hear the whispering going on behind your back. If anything that 2007 Tour was more bonkers than the 2006 Tour, which is saying something, there was so much going on. The last hurrah for the drug cheats some have called it. Let's hope so.

Back in 2007 there was the long-running saga of why the race leader Michael Rasmussen had

missed three or was it four drug tests in the lead-up to the Tour, and even confusion as to which country he had been in on the given day. That all came to a head in Pau when he was dramatically withdrawn by his team Rabobank, who were beginning to have serious doubts themselves, although I expect they were being leaned on heavily by the Tour organisation. Apparently Rasmussen finally admitted the true facts of the case to Rabobank's manager Theo de Rooij.

Rasmussen had been going well, in fact he had ridden brilliantly to win that dramatic stage up the Aubisque after which we were kicked off the Tour. He was in yellow and looking like a possible winner although he might have struggled in the final time-trial stage in Cognac. It was probably ASO's (Amaury Sports Organisation, which runs the Tour) worst nightmare if it subsequently emerged

that the yellow jersey and winner of the 2007 Tour de France had been up to no good and could offer no explanation for all those missed tests. After the Landis affair they were being ultra-vigilant.

Earlier on the rest day in Pau three years ago Vino finally got done for blood doping the same evening, dating back to the time-trial in Albi a few days earlier, a stage I had really wanted. I had finished fifth at the end of a dirty wet day with another drug cheat from Kazhakstan, Andrey Kashechkin just ahead of me in fourth place. You can imagine my feelings when it all came out.

What do you do? Everybody expects me to rage about it and tear my hair out but how is that going to benefit me and my career? You can either spend your life being bitter and twisted and becoming the victim, or just try and rise above it all and get on with it.

Yep, it all tends to kick off in Pau, but at least
today is quiet and the Tour seems asleep. The calm
before the storm perhaps, but calm nonetheless.
I think Andy Schleck has been doing some press,
I saw a bit on the TV a few minutes ago. He is
talking up his chances. He is a class operator in the
mountains and if anybody can make life difficult for
Alberto it is him, but 'cracking' him – no way. Put
your money on Contador come the Champs Elysées.

SIR PAUL SMITH

YOU would be hard put to find a bigger supporter of cycling in general, and British cycling in particular, than Sir Paul Smith, whose fashion label has gone around the world. Not least among us cyclists – we always seem to be wearing some of his gear and this Tour was no exception, with a consignment arriving to try on during the second rest day, at Pau, for the Team Sky end-of-Tour bash in Paris. Paul is a hard-core cyclist, in fact he initially intended to become a professional cyclist but had a really nasty accident in his teens and that was that. It was when he was recuperating that he developed an interest in fashion and design and the rest is history. He knows his stuff and keeps in touch pretty regularly with encouraging text messages. I read somewhere that he bought my old Giant bike from when I rode at Columbia. He has a high-spec bike at each of the four or five houses he owns around the world

and still goes out most days and puts the miles in. There is a pretty big link between cyclists and fashion chains in a lot of countries, especially Italy, of course, where the sport has always been synonymous with style, certainly since the era of Fausto Coppi, who always managed to look good on and off a bike. I suppose we are pretty good clothes horses, slim and fit and pretty normal dimensions. A lot of the guys like to look good as well, it's part of their persona.

COL DU TOURMALET

SO Alberto Contador has won this year's Tour de France, well – barring an accident or something very strange. He hung onto Schleck for grim death going up the Tourmalet and they virtually crossed the line together, although Andy just nudged ahead to take the stage. Just catching up with the relevant action now. Contador didn't really contest the stage win in the last 50 metres, he knew his work was done. Cosmetically, the race looks incredibly close, with just an 8 second advantage to Contador, but I think he has it all well under control. Andy must know it's not enough, he needed to put the best part of a minute into Contador to stand any chance. He is making brave noises and not conceding but I just don't see how he can win from here other than Contador being involved in and disabled by a bad accident.

It was a grim old day weather wise and by the

time we reached the Tourmalet it had closed right down – foggy, misty and generally murky, plus at various stages it chucked it down with rain. Miserable it may have been, but there was a Tour de France to win and only two riders contesting the issue, so it had a dramatic feel.

There were two category one climbs to negotiate en route, but although a seven-man break went up the road, there was never much doubt it would be closed down before the main event on the Tourmalet. Astana and Saxo Bank were fully on the case and never allowed the escapees too much leeway. Not that the two early climbs were a doddle. The last 3 km of the Col de Marie-Blanque are an absolute pig and fully lived up to their reputation. Still, at least we didn't see any bears up there. It used to have the reputation of being one of the last places in France to boast wild bears. Apparently.

they disappeared a while back so they introduced a whole load more from Slovenia! The Col du Souloir is never easy either, we know that. EBH and Flecha had got in a 7 mile break for us, but with about 14 km to go, as the mountain steepened, the main group were back together and it was show-time. The Tourmalet was the star attraction and, although you start going steadily up hill from about 33 km out at Adast, it's the last 10 km that really hurts when you ride West–East. In a sense you could say that after three weeks, and with nearly 3000 km already under our belts, the 2010 Tour de France was coming down to just 10 km. It was certainly a final throw of the dice from Andy and he forged on ahead but couldn't even begin to break Contador, who rode a foot behind his back wheel and never moved an inch. Interesting that he rode absolutely straight behind Schleck – never alongside or on the other side of the road, inviting a tactical battle. He was so close he could have been stream-lining in a pursuit squad. The way Contador was positioned, I suspect Andy would have found it difficult to keep an eye on him, although he would have sensed all the time how close Contador was. Also, Andy seemed flat out all the way, a classic do or die effort, yet in the past he has had alway loved to mix

it, easing back and then putting in a savage burst. He didn't seem to have the confidence to attempt that this time. Or perhaps he was accelerating all the time but Contador was almost reading his mind and reacting instantly. I wonder also what the effect of not having his brother Frank around is for Andy Schleck. Frank is a very talented climber and by all accounts the Saxo Bank master plan was always for him to ride for Andy at the death. It was always likely to come down to this last-ditch scenario on the Tourmalet – many of the critics and pundits have been predicting it for months. If you could have had the brothers tackling Alberto together it could have been very tasty indeed.

Today was the first day I have sat up on the Tour. Ironcially, I felt pretty good for once and could have gone quite a bit quicker – without ever challenging those up the road, mind, but what's the point? I need to conserve everything for the time-trial on Saturday. I eventually rolled home in the company of Mick Rogers, Maxime Montford, Lars Bloom, Jerome Pineau and a few others 23mins 19 secs back, by which time Contador, Schleck and Lance had all been interviewed live with President Sarkozy and were on their way back down the mountain.

TOUR CLIMBS

MY FAVOURITE TOUR CLIMBS:

COL D'ASPIN:

There is no real logic behind liking or loathing particular climbs but I have always loved the Col d'Aspin in the Pyrenees. I've been up it four times in beautiful conditions – which is unusual because it is one of those climbs often renowned for mist and fog – and felt good every time, so that helps. I like the twisty road during the forest at the start and I love the steady 6 percent gradient, nothing too dramatic or sudden. I love that 2–3 km stretch which opens out so it feels like you are riding along a cliff at one point, and I love the descent. It's not a giant, you can go at a good lick and it can all be over after, say, 25 mins, as opposed to slogging your way up other mountains for the best part of an hour. I am trying but really I can't find anything negative to say about the Col d'Aspin.

2. ARCALIS, ANDORRA:

This is another Pyrenean climb, a big one this time, which has been kind to me although I have only ridden it twice. The first time was a time-trial in the Tour of Catalunya and everybody was dreading it but I absolutely flew up it. Long and steady, set your gear and go to work, it is exactly the kind of climb that suits my physique and physiology. Then in the 2009 Tour de France, after a very encouraging first week along the south of France, it was the first big mountain stage and again I had a good one and established myself in the lead group for the rest of the race. Memo to Christian Prudhomme and ASO: can we have the Arcalis again soon, next time the Tour visits Andorra?

3. GRANDE BERNARD:

One of the highest and longest climbs in Tour history, yet an Alpine beast which I thoroughly enjoyed climbing when we went up it in 2009. It never gets too steep, which is good for me, and has lovely long sweeping corners as you get to the top; but it is the view from there and the descent that make this climb special. I'm not usually one to get carried away with the beauty of a climb, it's hard enough grunting your way up, but I will make an exception for this one. The view is staggering and the 25 km descent absolutely stunning and very quick. It's where Jens Voigt took a tumble in 2009 so you have to be careful, but this is one of the few mountain climbs where I will poke my head up and have a look around. Very uplifting.

MY LEAST FAVOURITE CLIMBS:

1. COL DE JOUX PLAIN:

A complete bitch of a climb. I spent most of a long hot day hanging on for dear life at the back of the grupetto in 2006 going over this bugger on the day Floyd Landis was going on his charge up the front,

when he made monkeys of us all. I remember thinking then he was going like a motorbike and now we know why. Meanwhile back in the grupetto it was horrible, horrible, horrible. But at least when we finally crested the top of the climb we could sit up and congratulate ourselves for getting up the final mountain stage of the Tour. It was all downhill to Paris now. Wrong. Some clown at the front of the grupetto went off racing Kamikaze style down the descent and fractured the grupetto to bits. Suddenly there was absolutely no safety in numbers. If we had finished as a group of 80 they would never disqualify us all, but if we came home in dribs and drabs we were in trouble. Us backmarkers tried to respond as best we could but faced an anxious wait before the race officials let us stay in the Tour. I think it was in Morzine, in the village the next morning that I had my Steve Redgrave moment and vowed never to race the Tour de France again!

2. PLATEAU DE BAIX:

There is simply nothing good to say about this climb whatsover. Boring, long, steep and almost constantly through a tree-line so with no natural features to aim for or at least to maintain some interest. I have ridden it during the Tour du Sud, when I was very young, and again in the Tour de France, and hated it both times. Would be quite content if I never had to ride it again.

3. COL DU MARIE BLANC:

There is no doubt that this becomes a very tough climb during the final 3–4 km, a stretch which is all above 10 percent, but there are harder climbs on the Tour which I get up more easily. This is just the mountain I don't cope with very easily and it seems to defy analysis – perhaps it's not a good fit for my riding style and physiology and I have suffered horribly on it. Andy Schleck has his hang-up about the Montée Jalabet, the climb up to the Mende Aerodrome – and for reasons that I can't logically explain this climb brings me out in a cold sweat.

ROOMING ALONE

ONE of the advantages of being the Team Sky leader is being granted my own room on the Tour this year. The norm on any Tour is to have a room-mate and I have been ok with that for years. It's a good way of getting to know your team-mates and bonding, and a good 'roomie' is a Godsend and can stop you fretting and help the time pass quicker. Steve Cummings is my ideal room-mate and at Sky they are careful to keep us apart because we are such strong mates that, in no time at all, we could become a clique, a little splinter group even within a small group of nine riders. To be honest, though, I am absolutely at ease with my own company and enjoy some peace and quiet in my own room. I don't get lonely, not a bit of it, and I don't fret. I phone home, talk to Cath and the kids, listen to my music and sleep. You don't need anything more. You are not up for anything more. You are at work and just

need to get the job done. When you are not working you need to be resting. It has always amazed me in the past at the Olympics, reading about some of our competitors doing the sights, taking in the local ambience, meeting people and making friends and generally chilling. What's all that about? You are at the Olympics to win gold medals. The moment they are over I want to get home. In the past I have brought one of my guitars with me – I think I drove Cav half mad at one Giro when we were rooming – but I haven't packed it this year. There are a few reasons why things have not gone so well this year at the Tour but my having my own room is not one of them. Time on your own is so important because there is so little of it.

WIGGINS

sky

BORDEAUX

Hotel Mercure – Bordeaux
Also in residence: Liquigas, Omega-Pharma-Lotto, Columbia

DONE and dusted, well virtually. Will treat myself to a nice glass of red later this evening. Let's see, I spent most of the afternoon riding past some of the world's great vineyards and châteaux – Clerc-Milon, d'Armailhac, Duhart-Milon-Rothschild, Grand-Puy-Lacoste, Château Lafite Rothschild, Château Latour, Château Lynch-Bages, Château Mouton Rothschild – so we should be able to rustle up something decent. I deserve it today. I don't suspect anybody noticed but I rode one of the best time-trials of my life and still only came ninth. As a ride I rank it right up there with almost anything I've done, but I suppose there was an element of too little too late about it. The critics have already

written this Tour off as a failure and weren't looking my way. I got very unlucky with the weather – again – when a strong blustery headwind kicked up down the Gironne estuary in the late afternoon – as some local experts had predicted – as I rode between Bordeaux and Pauillac, but this time there can be no recriminations or inquests. On the final time-trial you start in strict GC order with the lanterne rouge going first at some ungodly hour in the morning and the yellow jersey last out in the later afternoon. It's purely the luck of the draw in terms of the weather and the Gods were against us again. I rode bloody well though, the only one of the last 50 starters – the top 50 riders in the GC of the world's toughest cycling race – to make it into the top ten for the stage itself. Knowing that is a big morale booster for me. Certainly the guys in the final 20–25 would have been fighting hammer

and tongs to improve their GC ranking, so they will have been flat out and on the day I was the quickest of the lot. The guys who started earlier, including the final one, two, three – Fabian Cancellara, Tony Martin and Bert Grabsch – had it much easier and have been gracious enough after the race to admit as much. Deep down I know that was as close to Fabian as I have been in a very long time. He has been dishing out some real batterings in recent years but this was much better. Over a distance of 52 km, with probably 40 km of that straight into the wind, I reckon I lost the best part of 3 minutes to the elements and I eventually finished 3.33 down. I probably still wouldn't have beaten 'Spartacus' on a level playing field, but I would have made him sweat for once and, in my heart, I know that it was a podium ride and it could well have been nip and tuck between me and Tony for second place. That

is something good and reassuring to take away from this Tour because we are talking the world's best in those twc. Of those who started in the last batch in similar conditions, I was 3.38 ahead of Lance, a terrific time-trialler who excelled in the prologue back in Rotterdam and would have been looking to mark his last stage proper in the Tour with something good, and 2 mins 10 secs ahead of Alberto, who was riding for his life to hold off Andy Schleck to win his third title.

The battle for GC unexpectedly kicked off a bit, despite Andy failing to get the advantage he needed on the Tourmalet. Fair play to him though, he went off like a bat out of hell in his time-trial and at one stage had moved to within 2 seconds of virtual yellow on the road, with Alberto seeming to struggle a bit into the wind. A minor mechanical there or slight panic from Alberto at that stage

could have been interesting, but Alberto is a high-class time-trialler and managed to pull it together during the second part of the stage. He looked at the limit to me though, this Tour title was hard earned. He eventually got home by 39 seconds and of course the media had kittens over that! You already know my views on the 39 seconds incident.

It won't get any easier for Alberto in the years to come. Andy is getting stronger by the year as a climber and showed today that his time-trialling could improve a fair bit yet if he is prepared to work on it. The pavé stage was a big boon for him this year, unexpectedly so. He rode the Aranberg stage brilliantly and deserves massive credit for that, and I for one would like to see one of those novelty stages every year to shake up the GC in the first week. Andy does need to get a strong team behind him though. It's an open secret that he and

Frank are off to be part of a new Luxembourg-based team next season, and starting a new team is never easy and can take time. As for me, I'm still scratching my head. I can't get a handle on my form at all these last three weeks. I felt great today and although, like all the later starters, I had to work hard into the strong wind, I felt plenty of power coming through. I couldn't have ridden much better today. There was plenty left in the engine, and that's frustrating because, when I needed it at other stages of the race, it wasn't there. On Friday I got involved in helping the Sky train in the sprint – we were trying again to get that elusive stage win for EBH – and again I could feel a real surge of power and it was pretty effortless tapping the pedals all day. We did a really good lead-out actually and worked well as a team – you could feel something very good coming together but it didn't quite work

out for us and that man Cav took his fourth stage.

You dream of finding that sort of form. I think back to that Ravel stage when I was – and still am – kicking myself for not going with Vino. I had speed and power to burn but was locked into the team plan, a bit on autopilot if you like, when I should have been more opportunistic – and if I'm honest I was just plain confused by my form. I just didn't trust how I was feeling, which was bloody good. My GC ranking and middling form in the mountains said I was not in good form and my Tour was a failure, yet at various times I felt great and should have gone quicker.

Will mull it over with the Sky guys; we need to get to the bottom of it for next year. We are heading up to Longjumeau on the TGV first thing tomorrow before the promenade into Paris. I expect there will be plenty of banter on the train. Will see if I

can find Cav – and congratulate him on a great Tour. He certainly did his stuff again in Bordeaux, winning the sprint with loads to spare. Nothing seems to stop Cav. He basically freestyled it in Bordeaux, jumping from train to train – he latched onto us at one time, and even gave us a namecheck afterwards at the winner's interview! – and then romped away in style. He is some operator when his confidence is up.

13	26	PLAZA MOLINA Ruben	GCE	ESP	92h10'50"	12'02"	78	
14	24	LEIPHEIMER Levi	GCE	ESP	92h13'09"	14'21"	79	
15	61	KLÖDEN Andréas	RSH	USA	92h13'17"	14'29"	80	
16	9	ROCHE Nicolas	RSH	GER	92h13'28"	14'40"	81	
17	37	VINOKOUROV Alexandre	ALM	IRL	92h15'24"	16'36"	82	
18	133	LÖVKVIST Thomas	AST	KAZ	92h15'47"	16'59"	83	
19	85	DE WEERT Kevin	SKY	SWE	92h16'34"	17'46"	84	
20	91	GADRET John	QST	BEL	92h19'34"	20'46"	85	
21	107	SASTRE Carlos	ALM	FRA	92h20'42"	21'54"	86	
22	166	MORENO FERNANDEZ Da	CTT	ESP	92h22'52"	24'04"	87	
23	21	MOREAU Christophe	OLO	ESP	92h25'25"	26'37"	88	
24	31	ARMSTRONG Lance	GCE	FRA	92h28'26"	29'38"	89	
25	62	WIGGINS Bradley	RSH	USA	92h32'49"	34'01"	90	
26	121	CASAR Sandy	SKY	GBR	92h38'08"	39'20"	91	
27	174	EVANS Cadel	FDJ	FRA	92h38'12"	39'24"	92	
28	89	*EL FARES Julien	BMC	AUS	92h44'40"	45'52"	93	
29	201	RIBLON Christophe	COF	FRA	92h49'15"	50'27"	94	
30	58	CUNEGO Damiano	ALM	FRA	92h52'10"	53'22"	95	
31	131	VAN SUMMEREN Johan	LAM	ITA	92h54'01"	55'13"	96	
32	41	CHAVANEL Sylvain	GRM	BEL	92h55'41"	56'53"	97	
33	102	BASSO Ivan	QST	FRA	92h57'41"	58'53"	98	
34	93	AERTS Mario	LIQ	ITA	92h58'05"	59'17"	99	
35	194	GUSTOV Volodymir	OLO	BEL	92h58'21"	59'33"	100	
36	189	GARATE Juan Manuel	CTT	UKR	92h01'24"	1h02'36"	101	
37	118	VERDUGO Gorka	RAB	ESP	92h08'39"	1h09'51"	102	
38	179	ROGERS Michael	EUS	ESP	92h08'51"	1h10'02"	103	

CHAMPS ELYSÉES

Hotel Concorde La Fayette – Paris
Also in residence: AG2R Mondiale, Astana, BBOX Bouygues Telecom, BM Racing, Caisse d'Epargne, Cervelo, Cofidis, Euskatel-Euskadi, FDJ, Footon-Servetto, Garmin-Transitions, Katusha, Lampre, Liquigas-Domio, Omega Pharma-Lotto, Quick Step, Rabobank, HTC-Columbia, Milram, Radioshack, Saxo Bank

THERE is not much out there that beats the feeling when you finally race onto the Champs Elysées on the final Sunday of the Tour – 22 days and nearly 3600 km after you set out from the Départ. It's a spine-chilling moment and I know that, for many riders who are out of contention for the various jerseys, it is the prospect of that final hour racing in front of probably a million people in central Paris that keeps them going during the last week, when

it would be much easier, and probably sensible, to abandon the race.

To race into the city centre and then spend an hour charging up and down the Champs is a massive buzz, but it is also quite an emotional moment and catches the Tour debutants by surprise – it's a celebration of the fact that, despite everything, you have somehow made it around France and arrived safely 'home'. You can never overstate the physical challenge of the Tour de France: to complete the course at the speed we race and in all the climatic conditions and after all the crashes is still an adventure and a massive challenge. It doesn't just happen, you have to make it happen. It makes me laugh sometimes when people treat the lanterne rouge as a joke figure, the man who finished the race last three or four hours behind the leader in GC. Who was it this year? Let

me think, last time I looked it was between Bert Grabsch and Adriano Malori. Hang on, that still makes him an incredibly good bike rider and an exceptional athlete.

Everything hits you all at once on the Champs – relief at having got around, appreciation for all your colleagues and the excitement of being back with your wife and family within an hour of two. It's a real carnival atmosphere and somehow we all feel like winners, no matter how rubbish the Tour has been individually.

It's a long day though. We always seem to end up hundreds of miles from Paris on the final Saturday night, so there is a dawn chorus the next morning to get the TGV to the final stage start somewhere outside the capital. That final Saturday is also the traditional night for a bit of team blow out at meal-time, unless you are contesting the green jersey and the sprint the following day. It's a bleary-eyed trip for the peloton as we eat up the miles on the train and of course the first couple of hours of the stage are spent promenading along, which is designed to make time for the yellow jersey as he gets his picture taken with everybody and dispenses the champagne.

There was a funny moment this year when Andy Schleck went charging up the road and Contador chased – a re-enactment of their stage – and, would you believe it, Andy's bike went tech again. No, really. At first we thought he was joking as he motioned up the team car, but no, there was a problem with the chain again and he needed a new bike. Bit eerie that. It just wasn't meant to be this year, Andy.

Lance caused a bit of a commotion this time around when he and Radioshack turned up in

a new, non-approved, top with a large number 28 across the back and front. He was trying to publicise the fact that, according to latest statistics, there are 28 million people in the world fighting their own daily battle with cancer. It was a good strong image and message but officialdom wasn't happy – the gear hadn't been scrutinised and sanctioned, and there was a big stand-off and argument before Radioshack had to stop and change into their approved gear. Lance is canny though. The furore and all the cameramen chasing around meant that the 28 shirt and message got much more coverage than it would otherwise have done. I had to chuckle really, despite losing the battle Lance actually won the war hands down.

There is a myth, by the way, that the last day is a total doddle, but I can dispel that now. About 20-30 miles outside of the city the pace really starts

cranking up as the sprint teams jostle for position and the adrenalin surge as you hit the Champs is so huge that the last hour is always the quickest of the Tour. It goes in a flash. You are absolutely flat out and even if you are not in contention for anything you get carried away to a certain extent. This year at Sky we still had plans to try and get a last-ditch stage win for EBH and we worked our socks off, but to no avail – again; Cav did his normal trick of ghosting in from nowhere when the others weren't looking, and shredding the field. They all moved to the left as they exited Place de la Concorde and, just for a second, it seemed Cav might have got it wrong, but at that precise moment there was a blur of movement down the right and he was home and dry, and putting his palm up to the sky to indicate five wins.

Afterwards, it's great for an hour or two. We

crack open the champagne or just a plain can of beer and set off on a leisurely lap of honour, catching up with friends and family and saying a big thank you to all the British fans who stuck with us this year. The unstinting support was there right to the end and it was a big boost. We will return and do better next year. You stop and congratulate all the riders you can, not just your team, and all the tensions of the previous three weeks drain away. You have been part of something big together, even if you have ridden for opposing sides and spent every day trying to get the better of each other. It's quite a heady feeling. More than anything it was great just to be with Cath again and enjoy a beer and take it all in.

Slowly you make your way back to the massive hotel and already there is a feel of the circus leaving town as bikes are plucked from you and packed up in the vans around the corner. The massive foyer is a mad bustling scene, a flash of TV lights and cameras, as scores of family reunions and ad hoc press interviews take place. Everybody seems to be shouting and then the place goes completely nuts when the yellow jersey eventually arrives and is besieged by media and fans.

In the past I have gone off on a big one in Paris with the lads on the Sunday night, as all the riders let off steam. You can imagine the scene. Not that everything always went to plan. The year Cofidis got chucked out, 2007, on the Thursday night of the final week Cath was packing her bags and heading over to Paris for a spot of shopping for my arrival but had to cancel her plans as I stormed off out of Pau and flew back to Manchester in disgust. I booked us into a nice hotel in Manchester and we just had a big weekend on the town together by way

of compensation.

This year I was looking for a quiet one. Given that I hadn't exactly set the world alight it didn't seem appropriate to be celebrating as such; that wasn't my mood anyway, and Cath was over with the two kids – Ben and Bella – so after a very pleasant laid back team meal with Sky and a few of their guests it was off to bed. Three days at Eurodisney Paris awaits, which I suspect is going to be every bit as tiring as a day climbing in the Alps. But at least you can treat yourself to an ice cream at Eurodisney.

UNSUNG HEROES OF THE

YOU can pick up a paper or a book almost anytime and read about Lance, Mark Cavendish, Alberto Contador, Andy Schleck and a select few others. They make the headlines and the TV cameras seek them out every day in the bunch. They are, rightly, the most 'rewarded' of the riders in the peloton and, over the years, have taken most of the plaudits – but they also take the flak when things go wrong. In many ways they inhabit a different world; they are exceptional riders but there are many special riders in the peloton battling away every day, doing their jobs to perfection with barely a tap on the shoulder or a doffed cap in their direction. The unsung heroes – well, it's about time I outed a few of them, brilliant riders who flog themselves time after time and perform minor miracles without the wider sporting public even knowing.

1. STUART O'GRADY (Australia):

Stuey has been a very big star in his own right but because he just loves the sport and has no ego he has been happy in recent years, as he grows a little older, to bury himself for the Schleck brothers and others at Saxo Bank. He was at it again this year, putting in massive turns at the front for Saxo Bank and bringing back nine, ten, eleven water bottles at a time. He was doing just that in 2007 in the Le Grand Bornand–Tignes stage when he crashed – he fractured eight ribs, his right shoulder blade, his right collar bone, punctured a lung and cracked three vertebrae. Even he had to abandon that day, but he bounced straight back the next season. A broken body was never going to stop him. There is no ego or prima donna attitudes with Stuey – he has forgotten more than most of his colleagues will ever know about professional road cycling yet he remains

...OTON

the ultimate team-man at all times. You don't find many of those. Among other things, he is without doubt the toughest rider physically I have ever known. He probably feels the pain, he just doesn't show it. He never knows when he is beaten and has the total respect of the peloton. Stuey doesn't just seem to have been around forever, he has!

This is a guy who won a silver medal in the Team Pursuit on the track at the 1992 Olympics in Barcelona, that's the Games I watched as a 12-year-old schoolboy, when I got turned on to track cycling by Chris Boardman and his fantastic space-age Lotus bike in the Individual Pursuit. I've always identified with Stuey because of that track background – he won a couple of World Team Pursuit titles with Australia and a pile of medals at the 1994 Commonwealth Games. He was also in that Aussie squad that beat the England team I was

riding for when they broke the world record in the Manchester Commonwealth Games, and he bowed out on the track with an Olympic Madison title with Graeme Brown in Athens, a race in which myself and Rob Hayles finished third. He's a class act as well as having that hard as nails attitude. This is a man who has finished runner-up four times in the points competition on the Tour, won three stages and worn the yellow jersey. His greatest moment, though, has to be when he won Paris–Roubaix in 2007, one of the most popular wins ever. I suppose he will have to retire one day but I will only believe it when I see it.

2. ANDREAS KLODEN (Germany):
This guy never seems to get a mention, is always basically working as a super-domestique and yet he has achieved two 2nd places, a 6th and then a

14th in this year's Tour. It's only in the last couple of years that I can fully appreciate just how classy and consistent that is, given his other responsibilities – during that time he has ridden for Jan Ullrich, Alexander Vinokourov, Alberto Contador and finally, just this year, Lance Armstrong. I wouldn't claim to know him from Adam really, my only contact is a brief nod of recognition and quick hello every time a big prologue or time-trial comes along. You know for sure that on such occasions he will be there at the starter's gate, fit and very competitive. He keeps himself to himself in the peloton and famously doesn't do any press. I am guessing he is also a man that doesn't 'do' emotion, at least in public. He must be a great colleague to have alongside you. Rock solid. It was very classy this year when, like me, he struggled initially yet somehow managed to pull it around. I can safely say just how difficult that must have been.

3. CHRIS ANKER SORENSEN and NICKI SORENSEN (Denmark):

I'm going to link these two together not because they are both Danish, ride for the same team and share the same surname but because to me they both epitomise the best in professional road racing. When you look at that formidable Saxo Bank team that has ridden for the Schlecks these last couple of years many see first the work that Jens Voigt and Fabian Cancellara do for them. I wouldn't decry their efforts at all but the Sorensens were both heroes for keeping their noses to the grindstone. Chris is a very talented all-round rider indeed, and is still young enough at 26 to emerge as the 'next big thing' from Denmark, a label he has lived with for a while. He is more than useful everywhere but very reliable in the mountains – he had a great stage win in the Giro this year and finished third in the Tour of Slovenia. Nicki meanwhile is nearly a decade older and a brick in all conditions and most terrains. Good enough to have won stages in the Tour de France and Vuelta, he is the ultimate loyal lieutenant. When either of these two hit the front for Saxo Bank you know all about it and suffer accordingly.

4. STÉPHANE AUGÉ (France):

There are those out there who think Stéphane Augé is a bit of a pest but I've always had a soft spot for him since we rode together at Credit Agricole and Cofidis. On a quiet day, when the peloton is looking to rest their limbs and only go to work in the final hour, you can rest assured Stéphane will shoot off on a break. We will all curse him loudly but secretly I have always admired him; he is exactly what a bike racer should be. Stéphane gives it 100 percent gas all the time, he is a sponsor's delight. He will always do something to ensure a little TV time and press coverage. Stéphane is always getting a combativity award or nicking a few days in a King of the Mountains award early in the Tour before the big climbs have been reached. As a rider he hasn't got the class and the physical capabilities of some of the other French riders, such as Sylvain Chavanel, but my God Stéphane punches well above his weight. That bike rider's mind is always looking to get something out of the day. Life is never boring with him around.

5. BERT GRABSCH (Germany):

If you look down the Classement Général list for 25 July this year, after we finished in Paris, you will see in 169th position number 113 Bert Grabsch from HTC-Columbia, whose overall time was some 4 hours 23.01 mins behind Alberto Contador. But for Italy's Adriano Malori from the Lampre team finishing a further 4 minutes adrift he would have taken the lanterne rouge. The casual observer might be excused for thinking Bert was something of an also-ran, but I can assure you that if the ASO or somebody were dishing out MOM awards for the 2010 Tour de France he would be right at the top of the list. Grabsch is like the Sorensens in that his work often gets done, unnoticed, in the first half of a stage, away from the cameras and sometimes away from the drama of the day. We all know about Cav's lead-out train in recent years – those at the sharp end like Mark Renshaw, Bernie Eisel and Tony Martin who pave the way at the end – but for me that HTC-Columbia train gets under way

miles back down the line when Bert buries himself at the front of the peloton pulling back the day's break. It would probably be a toss-up between him and Stuey at the end of a Tour who has clocked up the most kilometres at the front. Again, it takes a humble man to do this, because he is a former World Time-Trial champion in his own right. He knows his job though, and he also knows that he is appreciated by the team and by Cav himself. He takes a professional pride in doing his job and, like all my unsung heroes, he does it supremely well.

6. CHRISTIAN VANDE VELDE (U.S):

Along with my Sky colleague Michael Barry, VDV is probably the nicest and sanest man in the entire peloton, somebody I admire just as much for being the bloke he is as well as being an exceptionally talented bike rider. He is an individual you can totally believe in and trust, a man of great integrity, and when he came 5th in the 2008 Tour de France – later upgraded to 4th when Bernard Kohl was done for drugs – I found his performance and approach very inspirational. After my 2006 and 2007 Tours – which were awash with drug controversies and deeply depressing for those of us who care about the sport – it was a breath of fresh air to see VDV do so well in 2008, when I was off the Tour busy preparing for the Olympics. I took heart from that;

saw me morph from a mere participant in the Tour de France (in 2006–7) into a rider who tried to race and compete for the three weeks. When I moved to Garmin-Transistions, where he was the GC rider, he offered nothing but support and encouragement; in fact he did more than anybody to help foster my own GC dream. There was no sense of him feeling under pressure or threat, he gives the team and his team-mates 100 percent all the time. Never was that more obvious than in 2009 when we turned up to the Tour with VDV our GC hope, although he was short on racing after a serious injury, while I was pencilled in as a super-domestique. To cut a well known story short, I had a good opening ten days or so and suddenly I was seemingly our best GC bet. VDV didn't bat and eyelid and buried himself every day on my behalf, rode by my side giving invaluable advice and generally guided me through the entire experience of conducting a race high up in the GC. It takes a very 'big' man to do that with a fellow athlete – I know plenty who would have suddenly found an excuse to be off the pace and back with the grupetto. Christian has done just about everything in his time: ridden for Lance at US Postal, ridden for Frank Schleck and Carlos Sastre at CSC. But for injuries at bad times in his career greater honours might have come his way, but in terms of an individual setting the tone for a team

MICHAEL BARRY

I COULDN'T let any book featuring the 2010 Tour de France pass without an appreciation of my trusted wing man Michael Barry. Just about the best thing of this opening season on the road with Sky has been riding with, and getting to know Mike. Along with Christian Vande Velde he is the undoubted gentleman of the peloton, a man who never lets his standards of behaviour and decency slip when the going gets tough. It was a pleasure, Mike.

Mike had previously done the Giro and Vuelta and it was surprising to realise that he hadn't ridden the Tour and that, at the age of 34, he was effectively a 'rookie'. Not that you would ever know – he was to the manor born and he rode wonderfully in support of me. It wasn't his fault that I wasn't quite firing on all four, but we will have another bash next year when we will try to do better.

Mike knows his way around the peloton like few others, knows exactly where to be to keep out of trouble, when it's time to move up, when to stay put, when to really switch on and when to relax. Or rather when I can relax. The great luxury of riding with Mike is that, to a certain extent, I can let him do all the thinking and decision making and, for a short while, I really can ease off mentally. He is in charge, I just follow him.

Mike is one of the most intelligent men I have ever met, both in an academic sense and a bike savvy sense, and it is an absolute delight just to sit back with him sometimes and talk bikes and road cycling. His all-round knowledge of the sport is almost exhaustive and he has well-thought-out theories on almost everything. And Mike has a great way with words, either in conversation or when he puts pen to paper – he writes acclaimed occasional columns for the *New York Times* – or when he gets his laptop out and fires off one of his insightful blogs on his website, Le Metier, in which he explores every aspect of the sport.

He has written a couple of highly rated books as well. One is called *Inside the Postal Bus*, which, in part, is his account of his years with that team when Lance was beginning to become a world figure. Fascinating stuff. His classic book though, which I frequently find myself flicking through, is simply entitled *Le Metier*, the same as his website. I'm not sure what the exact translation is from French – I think it's along the lines of 'vocation' – a job or profession that you are almost born into and feel compelled to undertake. In the book he basically charts his life as a cyclist for a year with HTC-Columbia in 2009 and everything is beautifully photographed by Camille J. McMillan. I love it in the way I enjoy the quarterly magazine *Rouleur*, which has the same love of pictures and rummaging around behind the scenes.

Our guilty pleasure on the Tour this year was to watch the *La Course en Tête* DVD – the Eddy Merckx story – with another video on the 1974 Giro. Brilliant footage, bike racing in the raw and, of course, the greatest of them all, Merckx ripping the opposition to pieces. No radios, hardly any sponsors' logos, no helmet, retro heaven. Eddy Merckx is often around the circuit – he was following the Tour this year – and almost always stops for a chat. It's strange to match up such an amiable down-to-earth figure with the slightly aloof 'untouchable' Merckx who appears in the old footage. Of course he was in full racing mode then, the greatest winner and racer of all time, going about his business, determined not to be distracted.

Mike has to be the most even-tempered bloke I know. At the end of the day in the team hotel you wouldn't be able to tell whether we had just endured a nightmare and suffered for six hours in the mountains or enjoyed a breeze of a day. Totally unflappable. What a quality that is to have. We went through a fair bit together this season and became a pretty close unit. The Giro was a heck of a race looking back – in fact physically it was probably harder still than the Tour – and that really pulled us altogether quickly. Despite everything, we had a great laugh on the Giro and, at the end of the Tour, when we were finally relaxing in Paris, Mike rightly said that we had lost that a little bit on the Tour and we should get our sense of humour and the ridiculous back a bit in 2011. He's right. Of course

the pressure was on this year – we so wanted to do well – but in future we need to keep it normal and remember to chill out occasionally.

SEAN YATES

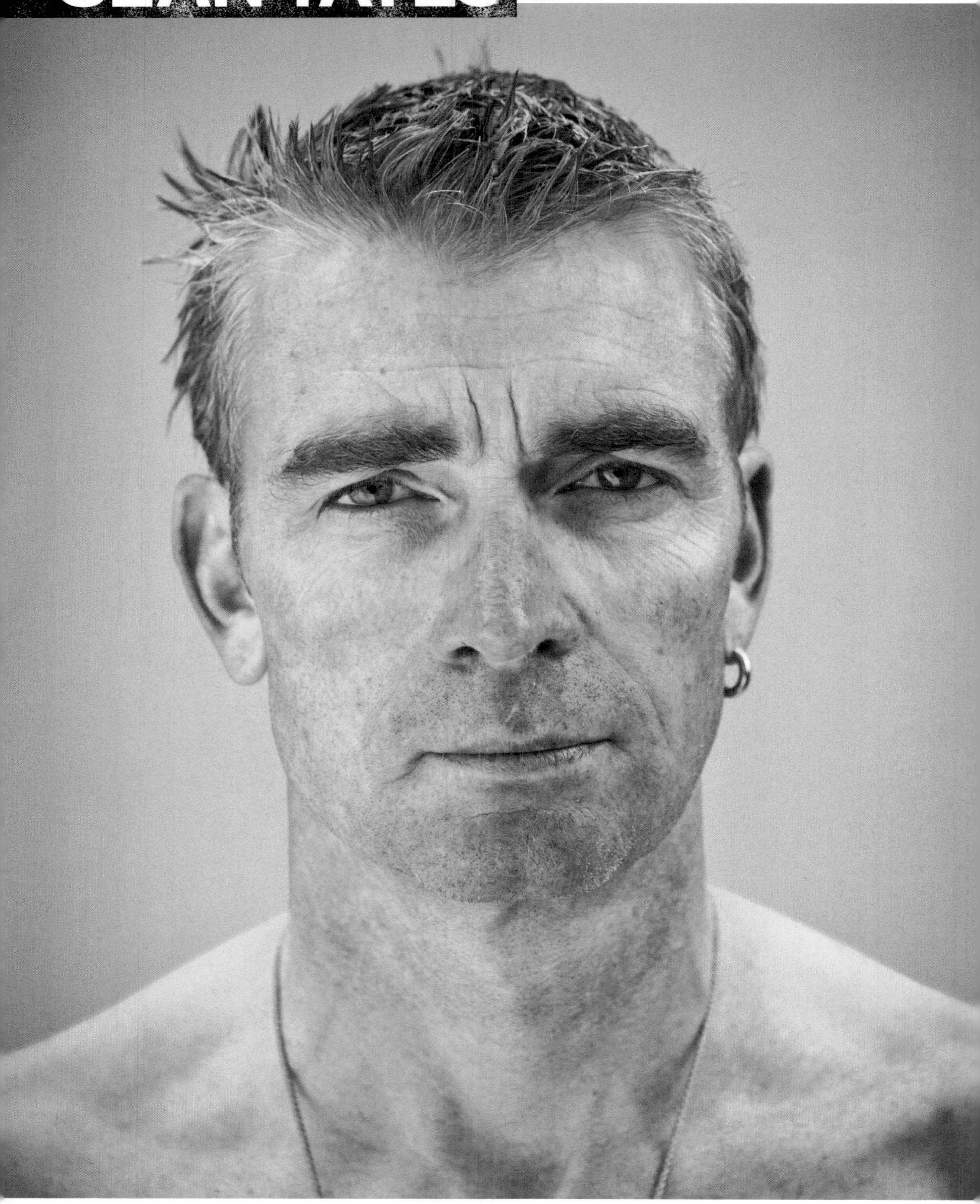

FOR any British cyclist of my age, Sean Yates was automatically our hero. A British hardman rouleur mixing with the best of the world every year at the Tour, contributing insane stints at the front of the bunch, chasing the break and setting the fastest average time ever on a conventional bike during his famous time-trial win from Lievin to Wasquehal in 1988 on stage 4. He even wore the yellow jersey for a day in 1994, his last full season. A phenomenal team man first and foremost, he took the young Lance Armstrong under his wing at one stage and taught him a few facts about life in the bunch.

What has been a pleasure and a joy riding in the peloton these last couple of years is to appreciate that Sean appears to be the hero for many top cyclists and camp followers throughout Europe as well. He is appreciated as much on the Continent as he is here. I have never heard a word against him and if you mention his name a lot of doors seem to suddenly open.

To me he was this brilliant time-triallist from Sussex who made it on his own in Europe and rode in a swashbuckling fashion that was really attractive. He held nothing back, gave it the full monty all of the time and would fight like a dog for his team leader. He also wore a stylish ear-ring which appealed to me at the time so much so that I had my ear pierced so I could copy him. The ear-ring defined him.

Chris Boardman was just as great a rider as Sean – indeed, in terms of medals and world titles he was clearly the more successful rider – and I came to appreciate Chris just as much in the years to come. But Sean was still my favourite, the heart-on-sleeve daredevil who buried himself every time, while Chris was the professor, timing his rides perfectly, squeezing out every last ounce of effort perfectly.

Sean was much more rock and roll. Lance in particular has acknowledged his debt to Sean for teaching him, among other things, how to descend properly at high speed. Being a big bloke in his prime – no matter how many pounds he lost on his latest crash diet Sean was bigger and heavier than most in the bunch – he could struggle up a steep climb and he had to make good the lost time by coming down the mountain like a bat out of hell. He did that in his own unique style, which was more like downhill skiing than the classic descending technique you are taught – with the inside leg leaning into the corner and the outside leg straight down hard to the pedal. Sean tended to grip the steel frame of his bike with both thighs and simply lean into all the corners. Fabian Cancellara does much the same now.

Sean was appointed as a directeur sportif (DS) for Sky at the start of the year and has been a great boon to the team. I've loved working with him. Before joining us he had first worked as a DS with Linda McCartney racing, where he had actually signed me – the chance to work with the 'great' Sean Yates was the main reason I went – after the 2000 Olympics in Sydney. Unfortunately the team went bust a few weeks later and everybody quickly went their separate ways again. He moved to the Aussie squad iteamNova and then on to two giants of the sport in CSC and Discovery, where he was reunited with Lance. He worked with Lance again when he was at Astana in 2009. What Sean doesn't know about the Tour de France is scarcely worth knowing. Been there, done it, got all the T shirts. And they still fit, so lean and fit is Sean, despite being the wrong side of 50 these days. He is famously quiet and laid back, which is a godsend in the madness, with everybody either on a massive high or down in the depths of despair. He uses the same tone of voice when discussing both. He doesn't try to dominate conversations but I have quickly learned to start switching on when he talks because he only contributes when he has got something worth saying. With Sean sometimes you have to read between the lines. He is so modest and he will never start doing the old soldier act, telling you how it was in his day and what he would have done. Nor will he actually criticise you outright, well – not in public or at a team meeting. But he will quietly make his point. 'Perhaps next time Brad we could do it this way,' or 'Well I suppose the other thing you could have done Brad was ...' Phrases like that mean it's time to start listening because Sean is about to tell you how it almost certainly should have panned out. He was terrific on this year's Tour, a great support who didn't start losing it when things didn't go so well. He was the same person – morning and night, good or bad. He has seen it all and knows that it only needs a couple of little things to be wrong and a spot of bad luck and suddenly you will be out of contention. It doesn't mean you are suddenly a bad rider, nor does it mean you are not busting a gut, it just means that this year it's not working out for you. For the vast majority of the world's very best riders, in any given year, the Tour de France doesn't quite work out for them. You have to deal with it. Sean is going to be a vital man for us at Sky going forward. He has the knowledge and he has the respect around the cycling world.

THE TWIG

MAKING the weight and living with the fatigue of putting in a marathon effort on virtually a daily basis for three weeks is such a fact of life in pro-cycling that it was quite a shock to register other people's surprise at some of Scott's pictures showing my emaciated body towards the end of the Tour or at the end of a gruelling stage. Cycling on a big tour is the ultimate endurance sport and you have to find a way of coping, whether you are a marathon man or not. And it's an equation you have to work out for yourself by trial or error over the years. You need to shed weight and get 'skinny' to make an impression in the mountains, but that needs to be fat you are shedding not muscle. Shed too much and you lose your power on the flat and in time-trials – and in fact the power you sometimes need on those long steady climbs which don't ramp up too steeply. That's why some commentators describe it as an art as well as a science; get the equation slightly wrong and your performance dips markedly.

As is pretty well documented, my 4th place in

the Tour came after I shed about 5 kilos of weight in the previous six or seven months to get down to a fighting weight of 71 kg. I did it slowly and sensibly, no crash dieting, healthy eating and the realisation that I should take it easy on the beer not only because of the calories involved but also because I am actually mildly allergic to beer; it bloats me up and the water retention adds a few kilos to my weight. Ever since then wine is my occasional tipple, except for end-of-Tour blow-outs. I seemed to get it just right in 2009. My weight was down but I still felt strong.

This year something wasn't right. Perhaps it was the altitude problem I have alluded to, but perhaps also there was something different and not quite right about the way in which I made the weight. Fatigue is a funny thing and to an extent depends on what you are racing for. This year I couldn't live with the front runners; as soon as they applied the pressure at the top of a high climb I couldn't go with them. Yet over the three weeks I didn't suffer like those trying to make the cut every day. I was in that middle ground – simply not able to match the very best on the day but some way ahead of the rest of the bunch. I remember very well those tough days at the back in 2006 and 2007, when just getting around was the only real objective. Riding the Tour is never easy but the fatigue is deceptive.

After a pretty torrid first week and then falling out of contention in the second week, I started to feel very strong again towards the end of the third week. I would have been perfectly happy for the Tour to have continued for a fourth week, I felt that good. But the moment the Tour stops the mind switches off even if the body is still madly revving away craving action. The engine still wants 5000–6000 calories poured into it every day but you aren't riding any more to burn those calories off. A week after the Tour I would start feeling completely exhausted – a sort of hunger knock I suppose after a modest breakfast – just walking around the shops with Cath and kids. I would suddenly feel the need to head for a siesta. And then the fatigue gradually seeps through into the system and hits you hard. I

am full of admiration for riders who prolong their season after the Tour; that is a major effort. I did it in 2009 but it was hard. I set my sights on the World Time-trial Championships in Mendrisio and actually did ok – I was third on the road when my bike packed up on me – but it was a major effort to keep going. Amongst other things, you pour so much emotional effort into the Tour that you feel just empty and drained at the end. You feel like you have nothing much else to give.

HIGHS & LOWS

BEST EVER DAY ON TOUR

2009 STAGE 15 – Pontarlier to Verbier 207.5 km
THERE were all sorts of reasons why this should not have been a great day. We had all got tired and wet the day before in a tough long stage and, leading into this big day in the Alps, everybody out there in the press and media seemed to be wondering if I could really keep my form up. Ok I had nudged my way through the Pyrenees all right but surely I would be found out in the Alps was the general conclusion. Well, wonderful to relate, I woke up on the appointed morning with great legs, felt superb. It all cracked off during the first hour and a half but I found I could react to anything with ease. Why can't you feel like that all the time? Up the final climb only Alberto Contador – making his big move of the Tour really – and Andy Schleck really had the beating of me. Among all the others I was ultra-competitive. Vincenzo Nibali and Frank Schleck got away by a second at the end, but I crossed in 5th and moved to 3rd in GC. Great climbers like Carlos Sastre, Lance and Cadel Evans were struggling home behind me. It was a surreal day. A lot of the time I rode neck and neck with Lance and I had to look over a few times to make sure I was believing what I was seeing. Me, Brad Wiggins, alongside the legend, going up a big Alpine climb in the lead group of the Tour de France and giving as good as I got. In fact better than that. At the end I squeezed it a bit and put 29 seconds into Lance and finished the day just 9 seconds behind him on GC.

WORST DAY ON TOUR

MY worst day ever on a road bike has to be stage 10 of the 2006 Tour de France which was effectively the first mountain stage of my first ever Tour. Was I in for a wake up call? Up until then I had just about been hanging on but thinking I could handle this Tour lark and get around ok. A nice gentle prologue in Strasbourg, seven flattish stages – all ridden full pelt at a constant pace I had never encountered before in a stage race – and one testing stage into Valkenburg, but nothing dramatic. Oh, and a rest day. I was pretty ragged but surviving when we lined up in Cambo des Bains for the first mountain stage. On paper it was tough enough without appearing to be an epic – the HC (hors catégorie) Col du Soudet and then the Marie Blanque before the descent into Pau – but I suffered from dawn to dusk. God I suffered. It was hot, I didn't have my climbing legs and the peloton sprinted from the off like it was a 4 km pursuit race. In no time we were strung out and, from the bottom of the Soudet onwards, I was consistently the last man in the grupetto, the last man in the Tour de France with the broom van hovering in the back to sweep me up should I abandon. I thought about it more than once and it was a very long day. Up the final climb – and I probably date my hatred of the Marie Blanque to this day – I was drifting off the back again and found myself with the team cars. Sean Yates it was – he must have been working for Discovery then – started encouraging me and said I was only 30 seconds off the grupetto; he said I could make it back if I worked slow and steady. But I had to start working now. I did it, just, and virtually collapsed half-dead across the line in Pau only to be greeted by journalist Paul Kimmidge who seemed in urgent need of a long exclusive interview about my first Tour. At that precise moment I could only think of two words but they were enough.

TXEMA GONZALEZ

JUST as we are completing this book has come the shocking news that our Team Sky soigneur Txema Gonzalez has died suddenly of septicaemia on the Vuelta Espana following an episode of food poisoning. He fell ill at the same time as many of the lads went down with food poisoning after the second stage but apparently it is nothing to do with that, it is completely unrelated, a terrible one in a million chance. He fell into a coma in the hospital in Seville and died soon after. He is married, with one young child I believe. And he was just 43 with a long life ahead of him. I am speechless, he was the nicest man in the world and a brilliant soigneur who took great pride in his profession and great care of riders. He was helping to build the team spirit that every new squad needs and there is no doubt he looked on us all as 'family'. Txema joined us at the start of the year and teamed up with me

from the off. He arrived from Euskaltel Euskadi – he was very proud of his Basque heritage – and Saunier Duval, where I know Dave Millar rated him extremely highly and formed a strong friendship. He was my own soigneur and I could not have been in better hands in a difficult year. We worked together all through the spring, the Giro and the Tour. That's a lot of time together and he was a big part of my life. Txema was unusually calm and grounded in the mad circus that professional bike riding can sometimes be. If you wanted to talk cycling or mull things over he would listen and contribute intelligently – he was a talented amateur in his youth and had well thought out views on tactics and conditioning – but more often than not an hour on the masseur's table would pass without a single mention of cycling or the race I was competing in. We would talk about life, family, music, football,

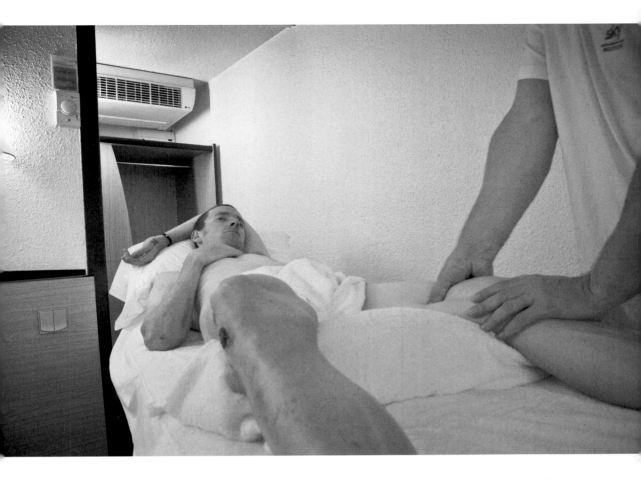

or sometimes we wouldn't talk at all. He knew the value of silence and the importance of an hour of peace in a hectic day. He could sense when you just wanted to be left to your thoughts or even doze as he went to work. He was a masseur who you knew had ridden a bike himself, so he knew all the sometimes forgotten small areas that get most sore and worked away gently, easing them back into life. I had a fair few crashes this year and he spent a lot of time keeping my body going. The term soigneur is a pretty loose and general one, and is much more than simply being a masseur or physio and a cheer leader. Carer is a better word and that's how the best soigneurs approach their job. Their task is to get their charge through to the finish in the best possible shape. I suspect many of them would make very good nurses. Txema was there for me every morning, making sure I had everything I

needed and massaging my limbs back to life. Last thing before I was ready to go out and face the world he would fix the miniature radio receiver and earpiece into my cycling helmet so I was in the loop for the day and in communication with the team cars. And he was waiting at the line every evening. I will never forget the scene in the bus after the seven-hour Queen stage in the Giro, when we arrived one by one, collapsed on the bus floor and he had to physically undress, sit us in the shower and force hot drinks down us. I received the news on the Friday afternoon before the national time-trial back in Great Britain and had to make the snap decision of whether to compete on the Sunday or head down to his funeral on the Monday morning. It probably sounds like an old cliché but I knew deep down that he would want me to race and that's what I did to the best of my ability, trying to make it as

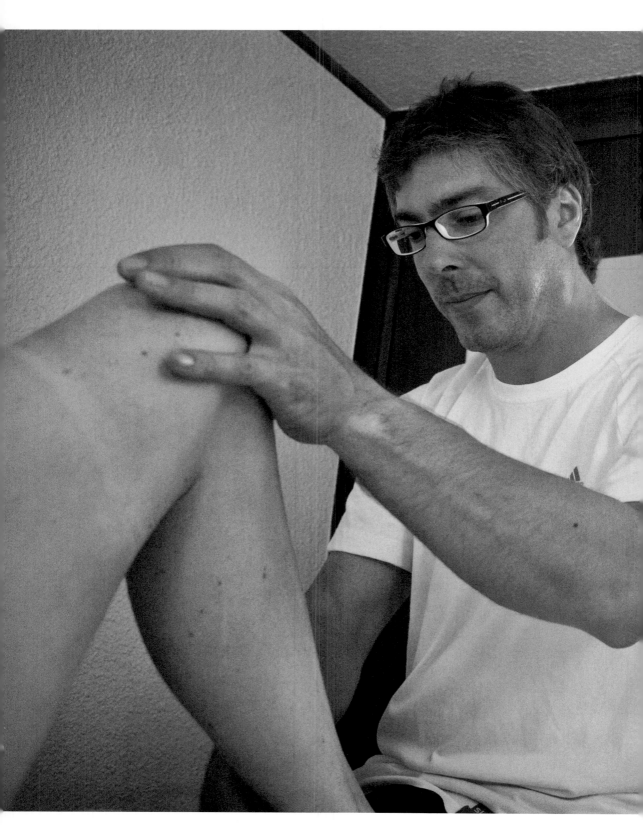

good a ride as I could. But that Monday my thoughts were very much with him and his family.

Apparently there was a terrific turnout from all the Sky boys who had been on the Vuelta – they withdrew from the race on the Friday night after they had been given the news on Txema – and the management. About 30 people from the organisation in all. Most of them drove up from southern Spain on the Sunday night to be there. He will be greatly missed and his death puts racing disappointments and petty hassles into perspective, as did the sudden death of my grandfather shortly after my return from the Tour this year. There is a much bigger, wider, world out there, and sometimes you need a reality check and a reminder as to what is really important in life.

KEEPING THE HOME FIRES BURNING

IT can be very hard on the road and some would say it's a life best suited to a single man but I don't know. It can be bloody lonely and dislocated as well as exciting out there, and it's a very unsettling, very dog-eat-dog environment sometimes. I'm not sure, actually, if those who cope best with the lifestyle aren't those of us who are married and have young families.

When I'm on the road, on the basic emotional level, I miss Cath, Bella and Ben very badly indeed. But, like a lot of sportsmen, I can go into a bubble for whatever period it is I am racing or competing. It's basically a form of denial. You have to do that – really concentrate on the Tour or the Olympics totally. If you don't, you will underperform for sure. Of course I will phone home first thing in the morning, and I normally phone again briefly right after the race to assure Cath that I am ok, and then, finally, the main call in the day, each evening when we will kick back and have a chat and hear about each other's days. But that's it. Sky organised Skype and stuff on the Tour for those who wanted it but I was happy just to make regular calls. As long as I am happy that Cath is happy back home I can concentrate on my racing and doing the best for all of us.

I don't delude myself. Of course it's much harder for Cath when I am away on a long Tour, which is basically a month if you take the week run-in, and even longer if we do a camp first. She is faced with the reality of having to look after the kids on her own throughout that period and dealing with the everyday things that come up in life for a young married couple with two energetic kids. She is left to hold the fort. But I reckon we both cope pretty well, in fact remarkably well. Cath comes from a cycling background herself – her dad was a former pro rider and she was a talented GB junior track sprinter before getting together with me. She knows the sport inside out and what is involved; she knows when I have to go into the zone, appreciates the need for hours of training, the discipline needed with diet and the need to rest when not training and racing. She never questions for one second the commitment I have to make and the sacrifices we occasionally have to make together. She is a fantastic support at all levels and makes it very easy for me to be a professional bike rider.

I look back to when I was on my own, single and trying to make my way in France, and I was floundering really. When Cath came into my life – I met her at a party after the 2002 Commonwealth Games in Manchester – things began to look up for me. After some hard years early on, cycling has eventually given us a very good living and Cath understands fully that it is my job as well as my passion. It is our meal ticket and gives us the lifestyle we have and the chance of financial security – hopefully for the rest of our lives. If that means me being away for months at a time on occasion then that's how it is. And it won't be forever.

Actually, although I've never done the maths, I expect I get to spend more time at home with Cath and the kids than most working dads of my age. When I am home in Lancashire I am truly at home, training on the local roads I know so well but with loads of spare time on my hands. When I am wearing my track hat and training for that, I get up early every morning and drive into Manchester but get back in the afternoon and evenings. We now also have a second place in Girona, where loads of riders seem to base themselves. I can put in some quality training there and Cath and the kids like us to go over during the school holiday periods. Love of family keeps you going in the tough times. There is no bigger incentive to keep going at the end of a long Tour de France than the prospect of seeing my wife at the finishing line in Paris and spending the next three days at Disneyworld with the kids. I do it all for them really.

CATH ON BRAD

I HAVE a very precious memory from the Beijing Olympics after Brad had won gold in the IP, standing with the British crowd singing our own version of 'Wiggo Wonderland' at the tops of our voices: 'There's only one Bradley Wiggins, only one Bradley Wiggins ...', blah blah, you know the rest. Truth is, there is not only one Bradley Wiggins. There's Brad the husband, who, in all honesty, is a bit of a dream to be married to: supportive, loyal, kind, generous, cooks, helps round the house, does the school run, never leaves the toilet seat up, washes my bike, pumps up my tyres (he's not a great mechanic but things are improving). He's a brilliant dad to the Wiglets, Ben and Isabella, and has far more patience than me.

Generally speaking I have Brad my husband from about mid September until about February, when a few tell-tale signs recognisable only to those close to him will betray the fact there's something bugging him. It's looming on the horizon like a storm and we know exactly when it will hit. His ears prick up when I tell him about race reports in the cycling press, and he pays increased attention to how his rivals are performing. Brad withdraws a little, loses his patience slightly more quickly, and starts to become more selective about what he'll eat for dinner. We can be sat on the couch after the children are in bed, I'll be talking shit as usual but whereas Brad will listen, Brad the cyclist has a sort of glazed-over expression on his face. His ears are closed and he's not heard a word – his mind is somewhere else. He'll get up a little more quickly in the morning and become more rigid about being on the road by a certain time. He'll stop wanting to come out for lunch or meet for a coffee. This is Bradley Wiggins.

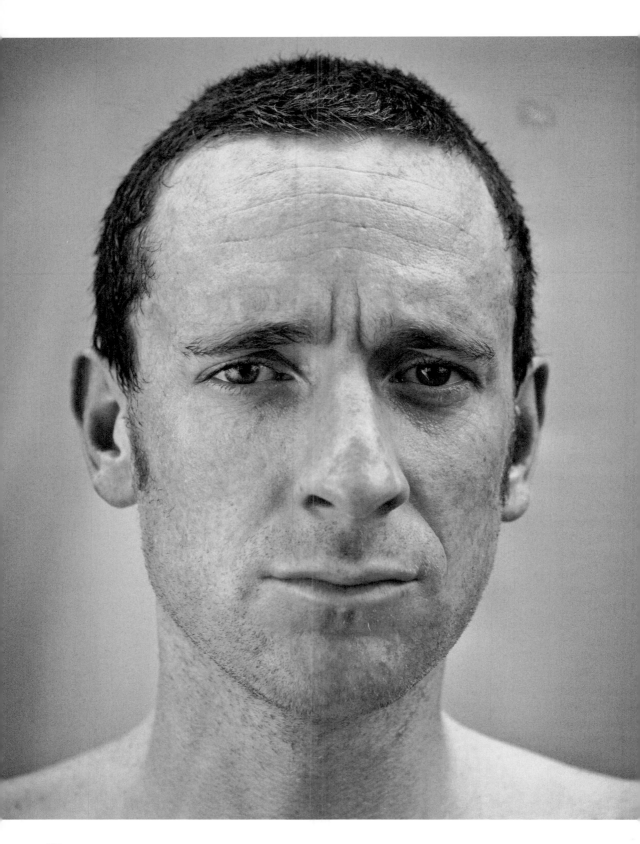

I have never known anyone like Bradley Wiggins – anyone quite as capable of focusing on a goal in such a way that excludes all distractions. It's like he's got blinkers on and doesn't notice the chaos all around him. He's so determined, so professional in every single aspect of achieving that goal. He's something of a challenge to live with when this red mist descends. He is infuriating at times, impossible to please and even more difficult to impress, although he's rarely critical of me or the kids. He withdraws into a metaphorical cave with his own thoughts and pretty much only comes out when he wants something. I should mention here that I am far from angelic. I don't feel like a long-suffering down-trodden wife, and we manage quite nicely. I bloody picked him at the end of the day, and I would again tomorrow. It was this bloody-minded determination and ambition that attracted me to him in the first place. I understand, I accept it has to be this way. It's not selfishness, it's focus, it's ambition; and me and the kids know we'll get our Brad back soon.

Bradley Wiggins was very different in the 2010 Tour de France. He was far from his usual upbeat self on the phone in the evenings; he seemed vulnerable, really sad. He was complaining quite significantly about the injuries he'd sustained in those five early crashes, the sight of which made me cry when I drove to Toulouse two weeks later for the rest day. You can see from the photos in this book he looks wrecked. The usual mischievous sparkle in his green eyes has gone out. Honestly, I can't recall an occasion in his career when he'd seemed so down as when I spoke to him after the Revel to Ax-3 Domaines stage, and he mentioned climbing off to gauge my reaction. I offered some really constructive and supportive wifely advice: 'Check in your shorts and see if they're still there, you're being a girl.' I didn't mean it. I was lying anyway; I wanted to cry down the phone at him and beg him to come home, then we could cuddle up in our little family bubble and shut out the world. It was hard to watch him try so hard and suffer; it was harder to read some of the reports, and

harder still to see some of the vitriolic hatred on the internet forums. I've come round about that bit: you can't make people like you, and an armchair opinion seems to me invalid, especially when given under a funky pseudonym. Truth is though, I've never been prouder of him than for the 2010 Tour. I think battling on this year and giving his all right to the end shows what he is made of; he was so down but never broken. A lesser man would have climbed off. He still thought he'd let everyone down, which is hard for Bradley Wiggins as he's a people pleaser. The rock star in him really enjoys all the adulation that comes with success. The kids find that bit confusing. At the bus Bella asked Gwilym Evans, the driver, was Bradley Wiggins in there, she wanted his autograph. Bella is generally ok with it, she sort of sees her daddy and Bradley Wiggins the cyclist as two separate things. Ben gets really upset; he simply does not understand why he has to wait in line and fight with everyone else to see his daddy, so will often have a huge tantrum, usually in full view and earshot of all the crowds surrounding the Sky bus.

This year it's taken a little longer for our Brad to come back. It's the first time in his career, really, that he has 'failed' to achieve his goal. He's failed on a huge stage as well, very publicly. I don't consider finishing 24th in the tour as a failure, I should add. I have an unwavering adoration for our sport and particularly the Tour de France – the riders are supermen. I hate saying 'fail'; it's not a fail it's a challenge – a test to see if you're worthy and tough enough to tame this great beast of a race. Surely we weren't so arrogant that we thought he was better than the greatest sporting event on earth, the biggest test of physical endurance and mental strength, that he'd beat it without a hitch? I know Bradley Wiggins is more than a match for this particular challenge in his career, and when he's recovered and emerges from his cave he'll be stronger and better. The Tour had better watch itself.

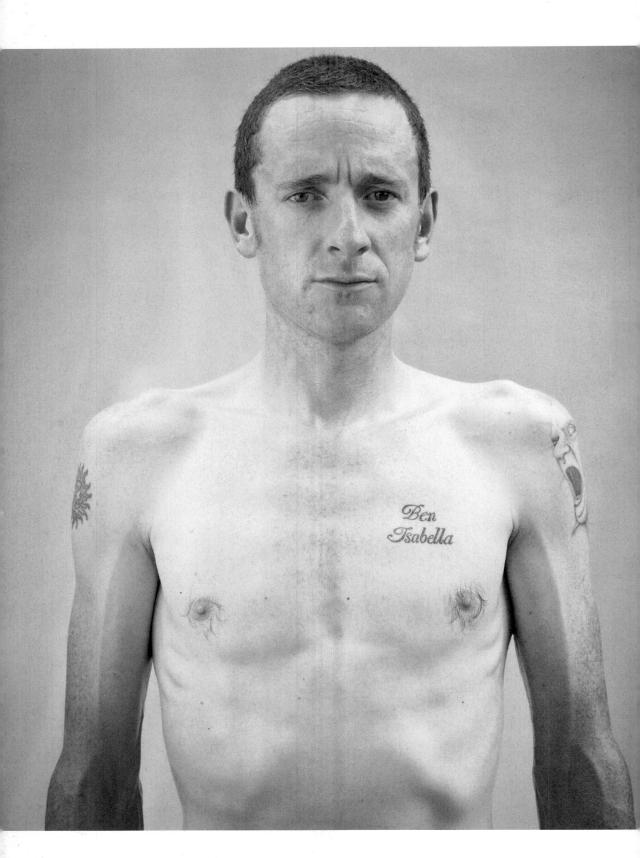